PENGUIN WRITERS' G

Writing for Busines

Chris Shevlin was born
grew up in Yorkshire, but moved south in 1999, ...
Royal Holloway, part of the University of London. He now
works closely with Clarity, the writing consultancy, and has
written for, trained and advised a number of clients from
high-profile companies. He is the author of *A Simple Guide
to Email*, published by Pearson Education, and *Cooking a Fish*,
a book of fiction.

The Penguin Writers' Guides

How to Punctuate   *George Davidson*
How to Write Better English   *Robert Allen*
How to Write Effective Emails   *R. L. Trask*
Improve Your Spelling   *George Davidson*
Writing for Business   *Chris Shevlin*

PENGUIN WRITERS' GUIDES

Writing for Business

CHRIS SHEVLIN

PENGUIN BOOKS

PENGUIN BOOKS

Published by the Penguin Group
Penguin Books Ltd, 80 Strand, London WC2R 0RL, England
Penguin Group (USA) Inc., 375 Hudson Street, New York, New York 10014, USA
Penguin Group (Canada), 10 Alcorn Avenue, Toronto, Ontario, Canada M4V 3B2
(a division of Pearson Penguin Canada Inc.)
Penguin Ireland, 25 St Stephen's Green, Dublin 2, Ireland
(a division of Penguin Books Ltd)
Penguin Group (Australia), 250 Camberwell Road,
Camberwell, Victoria 3124, Australia (a division of Pearson Australia Group Pty Ltd)
Penguin Books India Pvt Ltd, 11 Community Centre,
Panchsheel Park, New Delhi – 110 017, India
Penguin Group (NZ), cnr Airborne and Rosedale Roads, Albany,
Auckland 1310, New Zealand (a division of Pearson New Zealand Ltd)
Penguin Books (South Africa) (Pty) Ltd, 24 Sturdee Avenue,
Rosebank 2196, South Africa

Penguin Books Ltd, Registered Offices: 80 Strand, London WC2R 0RL, England

www.penguin.com

First published 2005
1

Set in 11/13 pt Adobe Minion
Typeset by Rowland Phototypesetting Ltd, Bury St Edmunds, Suffolk
Printed in England by Clays Ltd, St Ives plc

ISBN-13: 978-0-14-101677-1

Contents

Acknowledgements   vii
Introduction   ix
How to Use This Book   xvii

Part 1 *The Method: Planning and Writing*   1

1 About You   3

2 Your Readers   20

3 Your Goal and Your Message   31

4 Structure   38

5 The Medium   46

6 The Way You Work   77

7 Working in Teams   86

Part 2 *Your Writing: Making It Clear and Easy to Read*   101

8 Who: Making Your Subject Clear   105

9 What: Clear Actions   132

10 Getting the Tone Right   143

11 Getting the Length Right   159

Part 3 *The Details: Checking*   179

12 Tools for Checking   181

13 Punctuation   192

14 Rules and Conventions   209

15 Words to Watch   222

Index   240

Acknowledgements

I am very grateful for all the help and support I have been given in writing this book. At Penguin, I would like to thank Nigel Wilcockson and especially Sophie Lazar for their patience and good advice. Rupert Morris, founder of Clarity and a true friend, helped me immensely in all sorts of ways, too many to mention. Among much else, he introduced me to Max Leonard, whose considered reactions were extremely useful for getting the book finished. Finally, I would like to thank Sofia.

Introduction

Who this book is for

This book is for anyone who has to write at work. It is for all of you who write most days but have never been told how. It is for everyone who knows that writing more effectively could make a big difference to their prospects, their status and their usefulness. It is for everyone who wants to write more effectively.

In one way or another, most people these days are professional writers. If you're a marketing manager, an advertising buyer, an executive assistant, an auditor, a banker, a mechanic, a policeman or a temp, you're a writer. You probably don't think of yourself as one, but you are. As Dr Carolyn Matalene, professor of English at the University of Southern California, says, 'The literacy demands made on job-holders in the Information Age are extraordinary; they must improvise their way through complex writing tasks never imagined in their English courses.'

'Job-holders' pretty much covers it. If you're self-employed, if you work in an office, if you sell things, if you have to advise others, or if you're in academia, you are a writer. Whoever you are, in the course of your job, you almost certainly write emails, notes, reports, letters, forms, proposals, brochures, promotional material, CVs, and on and on. Many of the things you write go to people who can, directly or indirectly, affect the course of your career – and of your life. The impression you make on them with your writing will have a huge effect on their opinion of you.

Although you are a writer, you are other things too, and those other things take time. You have work to do, deadlines to meet, clients, bosses, colleagues and spouses to appease, and bills to pay. You probably lack the time, inclination and shelf-space required to plough your way through the innumerable style guides, thesauruses (or should that be thesauri?), acknowledged authorities on English usage, concise dictionaries of phrase and fable, and so on.

What you need is a structured way of improving your writing in as short a time as possible – so that you get the benefits without the pain. You also need a single source of answers to the questions you face when planning, writing and editing your work.

Why I wrote this book

It's easy for books like this to sound like lectures – dusty, cramped harangues from semicolon obsessives to deeply patronized readers. I hope this one doesn't sound like that, and I hope it's because I understand some of the reasons for people's mistakes and hang-ups about writing.

I work for a company that helps organizations to write more effectively – by training, by advising, by editing, or by doing the writing for them. We cover a lot of ground: helping staff respond to customers' letters of complaint; working with teams who write proposals for winning new business; and writing articles, reports and manuals along the way. I've worked with quite a few people now, and when I first started I was surprised by how badly people wrote. I have spent a lot of time thinking about why this should be, since the people we work with are, on the whole, very intelligent, highly qualified and often in senior jobs.

I now think that there are two main reasons. The first is simply that most jobs require people to do ever more – and more difficult – writing in less and less time. The second is that they're expected to do it without any specific training or preparation. I think this makes writing quite an anxiety-laden affair for most people.

In the sixties, seventies and eighties, teaching grammar was gradually abandoned. There was plenty of evidence to show that the way it was taught before wasn't very helpful, but abandoning it altogether has meant that many people now have no framework for talking about their writing. They have no way of saying why one sentence works and another doesn't, apart from vague ideas like 'flow'. While this may make people more creative, I think it can also make them more fearful. Most people realize that there are rules which good publications and writers follow, but they have no idea what they are, and no means of finding out.

This makes people unconfident about their writing: they have a nagging feeling that they are getting things wrong, but they don't know where to go for help. Specifically, they don't know where to go for help which they can easily apply to their situation. This leads to disorientation. Many of the resources that are supposed to help writers actually require a fair amount of expertise just to use. Most of the people who own a thesaurus don't know how to use it. In fact, most of them have never been told what it is for, so how should they be expected to use it?

The strategies that people employ to help them deal with their lack of confidence are often counterproductive. Very often, they make people's writing much less effective than it would have been without them. These strategies include:

- *Publish and Be Damned*. Write as fast as you can (usually right up to the deadline) and then send it off without checking it. Looking at it again would just make you feel bad, so why bother?
- *Make Yourself Incomprehensible*. Make things as complicated as possible – using jargon, technical terms and long sentences – and hope that people will assume that they are just not clever enough to understand you.
- *Write in Note Form*. Keep everything in bullet-points, fragments and notes, and deliberately avoid full sentences. If it's obvious that you haven't tried to write, then no one can accuse you of having failed.
- *Pass the Buck*. Do the talking and the formulation of strategy and leave the writing to others. Writing is a mere technical exercise anyway, like typing it up, so pass it down the chain of command to where you can criticize someone else for not doing it properly.

These are widely used strategies. They can work well as a means of dealing with the anxiety produced by having to write something. However, they work exceptionally badly as a means of producing documents that will reliably have the effect you want.

In other areas of life – especially in business – people are given very clear guidelines, but in writing we tend to give people gentle nudges, hints and tips, from which we expect them to work things out for themselves. One of the things that made me want to write this book was my experience in helping to conduct a one-day writing course for students studying for Masters of Business Administration (MBA) degrees.

These students were in their twenties or thirties and had all come from reasonably high-powered jobs. They were paying a lot of money to study so that they could go on to even more high-powered jobs. They were not aspiring writers; they didn't turn up with well-thumbed copies of T. S. Eliot's *The Waste Land* or Fowler's *Modern English Usage* under their arms – and why should they? They were, above all, businesspeople. They knew that being good at writing would be good for their careers, just as understanding marketing would be good for their careers, and they expected us to give them something that they could use to make an immediate difference.

For everything else they were taught, these students had formulae and protocols. From the SWOT analyses they used for strategic planning to the Ansoff matrices that predicted corporate growth, they had 'business toolkits' for every situation. When we turned up to teach them without one of these toolkits, their frustration was palpable. I could almost hear them thinking,

'Where's your matrix?' Afterwards, one of them wrote on the assessment form: 'If there's nothing to teach, don't teach it.'

But there is plenty that can be taught, and that people need to know. This book is my belated attempt to give those students what they wanted: a simple process that can be followed in order to make your writing more effective. Not necessarily more beautiful (although that may be a by-product) but more clear, direct, reasoned, comprehensible and structured.

There are a lot of people like those students. I know, because I have worked with them. In the course of my job, I often work from first drafts submitted by people in the client's company – from the most senior to the most junior. I began to keep an eye on these first drafts, noticing the patterns in the mistakes that people make.

It occurred to me that most people know enough grammar to get by. Problems in the mechanics of writing are usually caused by trying to squeeze too much in. But why this apparent urge to over-complicate? Gradually, I began to see that people had such difficulty with writing because they approached it in the wrong way – with no clear idea of who they were writing for, what they wanted to achieve or what they needed to say. Without any of these basic elements, they floundered, and they had to resort to elaborate means to hide their insecurity about what they were writing, and very often to hide the fact that they had no idea what they were saying – if they were saying anything at all.

I found that it was often possible to take someone from incoherence to something like lucidity just by asking a simple question or giving a concrete instruction. A department head at one big company seemed incapable of producing anything meaningful in documents pitching for new work. His drafts were always full of 'commitments to excellence' and 'ensuring the delivery of 110 per cent effort every time'. He could lard pages with empty, convoluted sentences that were incredibly frustrating to read because they took such a long time to say nothing. This is a very common pattern, and in his case it was cured just by imposing a structure on him.

We made up a list of things his department did, and for each activity I asked him to say how the prospective client would materially benefit in the first year of the contract and what the best result for a client had ever been. To a writer, this seems an obvious thing to do, but it had never occurred to this smart young professional who wrote as part of his job every single day and whose bad writing must have cost his company thousands of pounds. Once he began to write about concrete, specific things, his writing lost its sheen of unreality and began to mean something.

I started to look at the way my colleagues and I approached writing, breaking it down into a process, and trying to describe it in simple terms. I wanted to produce a single, short volume that would help my clients and other people in their situation. My aim was to write a book for those who do not intend to dedicate their lives to letters and words: those who just want someone to tell them what to do in simple terms, so that they can reap the benefits of being effective writers in the shortest possible time. This is that book. I hope it helps.

How to Use This Book

This book is divided into three sections, mirroring the process of writing: planning and writing, rewriting, and checking. Part 1 deals with the hardest and most important element. It gives you a method that will take you from having a blank sheet of paper to having a full draft. Part 2 deals with the writing itself. Once you have the words down, it shows you how to tighten up your sentences – making your writing correct and comprehensible. Part 3 tells you how to get the details right – including punctuation, capitals and tricky words.

Part 1   The Method: Planning and Writing

This section shows you how to approach any writing task in the most effective way – focusing on who you are writing to and what you want to achieve. The chapters here contain step-by-step guidelines and questionnaires to help you with particular parts of the writing process. At the end of every chapter is a summary of the main points.

1 *About You*

- Your writing habits
- You as a reader

At the end of this chapter you will know your own strengths and weaknesses, their causes and consequences, and what you should focus on when writing. This chapter applies to all your writing, so you only need to go through it once – but you may want to return to it to see how you've changed.

2 Your Readers

- Reader profiling
- Personas
- The situation
- What to do with the reader profile

This chapter will show you how to write for the benefit of the people who will actually read your document. It may be worth going through this chapter whenever your readers change – whenever you get a new boss or a new client, for example.

3 Your Goal and Your Message

- What do you want your reader to do?
- Your goal dictates your message
- What do your readers want?
- Managing multiple messages
- How to get your message across
- Telling your readers what to do next

Having identified your readers in the previous chapter, we now consider what we want them to do, and what to say in order to achieve that. This chapter will help you to come up with a series of key messages designed to achieve a clear goal. Apply the principles of this chapter to every piece of writing you do.

4 *Structure*

- Linking
- Explaining your structure
- Summarizing and reordering

You now need to assemble your messages into a coherent pattern. That means planning the structure of your document. This chapter helps you to move from preparation to fleshing out your piece of writing.

5 *The Medium*

- Letter
- Email
- Report
- Proposal
- Article or press release
- Brochure
- Leaflet
- Webpage
- CV

This chapter sets out the conventions for different kinds of writing, including letters, emails, reports and proposals. Here you will find clear guidance for each of the media you are likely to deal with at work.

6 *The Way You Work*

- Avoiding writer's block
- Looking with fresh eyes

There are a number of simple, practical things you can do to make it easier to get your words down on paper.

This chapter sets out good practices to follow when writing on your own.

7 Working in Teams

- Collaborating on small projects
- Working on major projects

For most people, writing at work means collaborating with other people – whether exchanging feedback with close colleagues or taking part in major projects involving many people. Here you'll find clear and effective ways of managing the process of working with other people.

Part 2 Your Writing: Making It Clear and Easy to Read

This section uses examples to show how to avoid some of the most common problems in writing at work. Part 1 showed you how to decide on your message and write what you want to communicate. Now you have words down on paper, Part 2 shows you how to refine your sentences to make them clearer and more direct.

8 Who: Making Your Subject Clear

- Introducing and explaining
- Making your writing less complex and technical
- If you're not sure what it means, don't write it
- Confusing subjects
- Sentences that don't focus on one thing

A clear sentence tells you who did what. This chapter focuses on the *who* part, setting out ways of making your writing more vivid and comprehensible by identifying who is taking action.

9 What: Clear Actions

- Padding
- Using the wrong word for the job
- Unnecessary, new or made-up words

This chapter moves on to the *what* part, describing ways of making sentences more dynamic and giving them more impact. That means identifying the essential actions in each sentence and expressing them as crisply and cleanly as possible.

10 Getting the Tone Right

- Sales pitches – the limits of enthusiasm
- Answering complaints – don't be evasive or impersonal
- Giving recommendations – the importance of confidence

Your message won't get through to your readers if you adopt the wrong tone. In this chapter, we look at the three situations in which people's tone most often lets them down, and discover how to give the right impression.

11 Getting the Length Right

- Giant sentences
- Stunted sentences
- Bullet-points
- Punctuation

Sentence length gives people a lot of trouble: too long and a sentence is difficult to follow, too short and it won't flow. This chapter shows you how to achieve a balance by breaking up long sentences and bringing stunted ones together.

Part 3   The Details: Checking

Part 3 lists the details that must be checked once your document is finished. It focuses on the most common problems and the mistakes that let people down when writing at work.

12 Tools for Checking

- Dictionaries
- Thesauruses
- Style guides
- Usage guides
- Grammar guides
- Other tools

This chapter looks at the different tools you might use for checking your work – including dictionaries, thesauruses and style guides. It gives some guidance on how to use them as well as recommending which ones to use – and which are available on the Internet.

13 Punctuation

- Apostrophes
- Brackets
- Colons
- Commas
- Dashes
- Exclamation marks
- Full stops
- Hyphens
- Question marks
- Quotation marks
- Semicolons
- Spaces

Punctuation is a vital aid to readers' understanding –
and it tells people a lot about how good a writer you
are. The rules are simple, so if you want to make a big
difference to your writing quickly, start here.

14 Rules and Conventions

- &
- Capitals
- I and me
- Numbers
- That and which (and the comma)
- They and he/she
- To boldly split infinitives
- Who and whom
- Beginning and ending sentences

Writing can seem to be full of conventions and rules
– such as when to use capitals – that everyone knows

but you. This chapter gives you all the rules you need to know.

15 Words to Watch

- Misspelling
- Difficult words
- Confusing differences between British and American English
- Jargon and buzzwords

There are plenty of words whose function seems to be to trip up and embarrass the unwary writer. This chapter gives you the low-down on the ones to watch, presented in alphabetical order. It also gives some differences between British and American English that are worth watching out for in the office.

Part 1

The Method: Planning and Writing

Here is my method for breaking writing down into a series of tasks:

1. Identify who your readers are.
   This is your audience.

2. Decide what you want them to do.
   This is your goal.

3. Work out what would make them do that.
   This is your message.

4. Set out facts and arguments to support that message.
   This is your structure.

5. Use the right words to flesh out your structure.
   This is your document.

But before you do any of that, it pays to know a little bit about yourself.

1
About You

Since everything you write depends upon you, it makes sense to start by finding out as much as possible about yourself – as a writer and as a reader.

Your writing habits

These questions might help you to identify some strengths and weaknesses in your habits. Answer 'yes' if you *tend* to behave that way – even if you don't always.

1. Do you plan or research excessively before you write?

2. Do you make substantial changes, either to your structure or to the way you've expressed yourself, after your first draft?

3. Do you read through your writing aloud (or semi-aloud, if you're in an office)?

4. Do you start to write before you are ready?

5. Do you think in detail about who your readers are before you start writing?

6. Do you write without a clear goal in mind?

7. Do you have three or four clear messages that you want to communicate when you write?

8. Do you – either before or after you write – make a plan of your writing?

9. Do you submit your writing without checking punctuation, spelling and sentence structure?

10. Do you leave your writing overnight (or for as long as possible) before checking and rereading it?

If you answered 'Yes' to questions 1, 4, 6 or 9, or 'No' to questions 2, 3, 5, 7, 8 or 10, then they are likely to be your weaknesses.

Weaknesses, strengths and overused words

By identifying your own traits, we can build up three written lists, one of weaknesses (or tendencies to watch), one of strengths and one of words and phrases you most overuse. Try to have about three items in each. In the weaknesses list, concentrate on things that give you practical problems (ones such as over-researching that mean you take too much time, for example) or that correspond to a part of the process on page 1 – such as not thinking enough about your readers. Each thing in the weaknesses list should lead to a specific action you can take, or to a variety of strategies you can try out. Don't put down things that will just lower your morale, like 'I'm no good at making jokes.'

Your strengths list doesn't have to be so practical, and it can include things that are straightforward morale-boosters, such as a nice comment someone made after reading something you had written. Your strengths list should give you a confidence boost when you're feeling low about your writing. It should also set out what your strong suit is, which may give you an idea of the safest way of approaching a particular problem.

It can be more tricky to identify words and phrases you use excessively – your friends and colleagues might do better at saying what they are. It's usually easier to spot someone else's most overused words than your own. Looking back over things you wrote a few months ago can help, as it feels more like looking at someone else's writing.

You may gradually notice your overused words over time, or someone might point one of them out to you. Just keeping a look out for them will make you think about your writing more. Once you have a couple, you should start looking out for alternatives to them. Whatever they are, knowing them will tell you something about yourself.

When Winston Churchill got a new aide in the war, Churchill gave him a list of his own most overused words and phrases, including 'vast', 'dark' and 'magnificent'. That list tells you more or less everything you need to know about Churchill's habits of thought and general approach to life.

Personality and writing

The kind of person you are affects the way in which you approach reading and writing. Alice Horning's book *The Psycholinguistics of Readable Writing* contains an interesting study of the ways in which personality can affect your reading and writing.

At the beginning of the study, the two researchers – Jensen and DiTiberio – gave readers a personality test which looked for certain character traits and classified people accordingly. The test, called the Myers-Briggs Type Indicator, is based on the ideas of the Swiss psychologist Carl Jung. It looks at four different traits, and assigns people to one of two personality 'types' for each one of those traits. The first pair of types are introvert and extravert. Introverts tend to look inside themselves and to be more concerned with what is going on in themselves than what is going on in the world, while extraverts are the opposite, paying more attention to the world outside.

The other pairs of types are more self-explanatory: thinking and feeling, sensing and intuitive, and judging and perceiving. Mostly, they are as you would imagine. Thinking types tend to process things intellectually rather than emotionally, whereas feeling types do the opposite. Sensing types rely on the evidence of their senses, while intuitive types rely on intuition. Finally, judgers make instant evaluations, while perceivers have a more open, less judgemental attitude.

Obviously it's best to take all of this with a pinch of salt. The tests (taken by two million people every year) tend to ask questions like 'Are you relaxed and comfortable in social situations?', to which the answer for most honest people will be 'Sometimes'. Nevertheless, I think Jensen and DiTiberio's research is interesting because it gives an idea of the different ways in which people approach the whole business of writing. See which of the following descriptions apply to the way you work:

Introvert and extravert

According to Jensen and DiTiberio, introverts tend to follow the recommended pattern: 'prewrite, write, then rewrite'. They work alone, and they don't get down to work until they're sure of what they're going to do. But, because they have planned ahead in such detail, they sometimes get bored with the writing itself. Extraverts, in contrast, like to talk their way through writing and to have some real experience to go on. Their ideas develop as they write, so they do little advance planning and tend to write very quickly. Extraverts find it more useful to make an outline of their work after they have done the first draft, rather than before doing it, and rewriting works best for them if they can talk to readers beforehand. Jensen and DiTiberio believe that extraverts write best about experience, whereas introverts write best about ideas.

Sensing and intuitive

Writers with a sensing preference like to have specific, detailed instructions, and usually focus on grammar and mechanics when it comes to rewriting. They present facts well, but may not have an overall framework for them. When they judge other people's writing, sensers look out for grammar, structure and explicitly stated points. They apparently outnumber intuitive writers by three to one. Intuitive writers prefer more general instructions, and like to have a lot of freedom in the way they approach a writing task. They write quickly, generating ideas and creating organization as they go. They are best at discussing theory, but they tend to forget about examples and sometimes don't follow the instructions they're given.

Thinking and feeling

Thinkers have a rather remote and impersonal approach to writing, and they, too, value a clear structure. In fact, they value content and structure over style, in contrast to feeling types, who like writing to be more personal. Feeling types like to get a reaction to their writing, and they like to feel that they are making their writing interesting and intimate. Obviously this carries dangers, and they can be sentimental and often deal badly with topics that require logic and objectivity.

Judging and perceiving

Judgers are good at meeting deadlines, and have a practical approach to writing, working through it section by section. They tend to be good at planning, although this can become a limitation. Sometimes they start writing too soon, before they have properly thought their piece through. Perceivers, on the other hand, can do well with a broad brief, but tend to find it difficult to narrow their focus enough to meet deadlines. Perceivers need a lot of time, and often do excessive research before they feel comfortable enough to start writing. They often write too much, without a clear enough point, and they can include too much detail and extraneous information. Although they are thorough, they tend to get bogged down in detail. When it comes to reading, judgers look for an answer, while perceivers want a thorough discussion. No matter what the content, perceivers tend to think longer pieces are better than shorter ones.

If you recognized yourself in any of the descriptions above, then you might want to update your list of strengths and weaknesses accordingly. Writing can be rather a difficult and lonely activity at times, but if you know what you tend to do well – as well as where you tend to fall down – then it might help you when you are stuck.

You as a reader

The way you write is also affected by what and how you read. Your reading style affects the way you understand words and the way you look for meaning, which can determine your attitude to important things like structure, logic, narrative and tone. So if you know what kind of reader you are, you can anticipate the strengths and weaknesses you are likely to have as a writer.

Reading speed and writing style

I noticed a long time ago that writers tend to be slow readers, and I think that this is because they are doing a lot with the words they read, extracting the full measure of meaning from them. One of the things they are doing is subvocalizing – unconsciously making small movements of the lips and tongue as though they were speaking, which allows them to hear the words as they read them. This makes them more sensitive to the tone and flow of a piece of writing.

This is not to say that writers can't read fast. Since I've been a full-time writer, my reading speed has increased enormously. It has had to, to get through the amount of background reading I need to do. But it has always struck me that writers have a slow and steady pace that they use when they are reading 'properly'.

In contrast, some of the non-writers I've worked with have very obviously had a completely different attitude to reading – and hence to writing. There's one who particularly sticks in my mind because he approached writing as though the aim were simply to put the names of relevant concepts – such as *government, community* and *technology* – near one another, padded out with smaller words. He had failed to notice that writing involves making points and communicating thoughts, rather than just listing names and concepts.

Dr Georgia Green, professor of linguistics at the University of Illinois, has studied this approach to writing. Dr Green's husband got her interested in basketball, and she began to read the sports pages. She soon became fascinated by the structure of the sports reports, which, she says, 'consisted of a randomly ordered list of facts about the game – who played what position, shooting statistics, point spreads at various junctures – interspersed among uninformative quotations from post-game interviews with coaches and players'.

She believed that the structure of sports reports

helped to explain why many of the students she knew did so badly in exams, no matter how hard they worked. It was because they expected all writing to behave like sports reports, which were all they were used to reading voluntarily. The result was that 'they were reading their textbooks as if they were simply lists of unconnected facts to be memorized.'

People who just skim for facts tend when they write to ignore the things that help readers most. They don't give you any headings to tell you what their writing is about, they don't build up logical points, they don't tell stories, they don't explain things. Sometimes they just give you lists of bullet-points. On the plus side, they tend to give you the names, numbers and facts you need.

But reading slowly can also have its downside. Slow readers can tend to overwrite, over-narrate and over-explain – almost as though they expect other people to be reading at the same pace as they are writing. If you are stuck at either extreme, it is a good idea to learn to vary your reading speed. Being able to skim is a useful skill to have in itself, but it will also help you to see the overall shape of what you have written, and to make sure that important facts and conclusions stand out. Being able to read slowly and to hear how the words sound will help you to get the sound, sense and flow of your writing right, and it will help you to punctuate more usefully.

How to read more slowly
There are three main techniques for slowing yourself down:

Read aloud, or try to hear each word in your head as you read

People who read too fast need to get back to basics. They need to hear the sounds of the individual words they are reading. The best way to do this is to read aloud. If this isn't possible then just allow yourself to mouth the words very slightly. What you're aiming for is to hear each word clearly in your head.

Stop your eyes skipping around the page

To stop yourself from skimming, you need to make sure you can't read ahead. A lot of people find it useful to cover the lines below the one they're reading with a piece of blank paper. This concentrates your eyes and your attention on where you are now. You can get the same effect by following the words with your finger or a pen: it stops your eyes skipping around and forces you to follow the lines of text.

Summarize each paragraph to yourself

People who skim-read often don't take very much information in. To counteract this, ask yourself 'What have I learned here?' after each paragraph. Try to keep your answer to a single sentence.

How to read faster

There are plenty of books you can read and courses you can take to speed up your reading, but just three simple techniques are all most people need.

Keep moving forward – don't reread
The standard way to speed up your reading is to cover the lines above the one you are currently reading with a piece of paper. This prevents you from reading back, which is one of the things that slows people down.

Move your eyes as little as possible
All speed-reading techniques operate on the principle that the less you move your eyes, the faster you read. Very slow readers look at each word in turn, fixing their eyes on it, recognizing it and then moving on to the next word. Each time your eyes move to a new position on the page is called a fixation, so a one-word-at-a-time reader might have 14 fixations for a single line. Speed-reading techniques aim to reduce this number of fixations per line. This means seeing more words in each fixation, so that you can read three or five or even a whole line of words at a single glance, without moving your eyes.

Don't subvocalize
Subvocalizing is basically reading out loud but with your mouth closed. Even though they aren't making any audible sounds, people who do this are still making minute movements of the muscles used for speech, such as the tongue and jaw. Making these movements can mean that you read about as slowly as someone reading out loud. The ability to do this is excellent for getting the flow of your writing right when you read it back to yourself, but it is also useful to be able to stop doing it. To make yourself stop, hold the tip of your

tongue between your front teeth and put one finger on your lips.

Exercise
Just measuring your reading speed is enough to improve it. Try doing 'sprints':

1. Mark in pencil where in your book you are starting to read from.

2. Read for five minutes (use an alarm) and then make another mark.

3. Note down how many pages you have read.

4. Count ahead that number of pages and make another pencil mark.

5. Try to reach that mark in four minutes.

6. Repeat steps 4 and 5 until you manage it. Force your eyes to move faster along the page and skip some words. Don't worry too much about comprehension yet.

7. When you have succeeded in getting down to four minutes, try to read the same number of pages in three minutes.

8. Then get down to two minutes – the important thing is to make your eyes move quickly and to understand something from the text.

9. Finally, read again for five minutes, as you would normally.

10. Note how many pages you have read this time – for most people it has increased already. The more you practise, the better you will get.

A Cloze relationship

Although people read and comprehend writing in different ways, readers have some very definite expectations of the way writing will behave. There is a kind of pact between readers and writers that goes far beyond simply speaking the same language. The closeness of the relationship between reading and writing can be seen from a simple test called the Cloze procedure.

The Cloze procedure was first used as a method of measuring a reader's ability. In it, every nth word is blanked out and the reader has to write it in. Poor readers find this impossible, competent readers put in words that just about fit, and good readers put in the exact word or a very close synonym. How often do you get to the end of a page and know the next word even before you have turned over?

Because good readers are able to substitute these missing words so well, the Cloze procedure has also been used as a test of how readable a piece of writing is. The more words good readers are able to fill in, the more readable the writing is said to be. The idea is that well-written writing obeys a set of rules which both readers and writers seem to know – even if they can't say what they are.

It is the knowledge of these unwritten rules that makes the difference between writing that seems readable and comprehensible, and writing that seems difficult and confusing. The unwritten rules are in addition to all the rules that can be easily written down and stated, such as when to give words capital letters. I have tried in this book to state as many of the unwritten rules as possible, but you need to bolster this by absorbing them yourself, and the best way to do that is by reading.

I believe that one of the best ways to get into good writing habits is to read well-written books. A good way to soak up the unwritten rules is to read a page or so of a well-written non-fiction book before you lay finger to keyboard. The rhythms of the prose will start to get into your head, as well as the explanatory style. This will also give you a feel for which words are part of the language of your profession (or your office: jargon can be very local) and which are generally understood.

The book you choose ought to be non-fiction because that is what you write at work. Fiction relies too much on characters' voices, which you won't be able to use in writing at work, and too much of fiction's effect comes from the narrative flow of events and emotions, which again are difficult to transplant into office writing.

It is worthwhile noticing the way good writers of non-fiction deploy arguments, ideas and information, the way they put people at the centre of their writing even when dealing with abstract subjects, and the way they make stories out of the material they have. The best example of this that I've come across recently was in a book called *The Articulate Mammal*, by Jean Aitchison.

The book is about linguistics, a subject that most

writers seem capable of rendering impenetrable and completely unreadable. But right at the beginning, Aitchison introduces a complex problem – how people learn to speak – by telling a story in which two protagonists, Noam Chomsky and B. F. Skinner, seem to debate the subject. Despite the fact that both Chomsky and Skinner are difficult writers talking about a difficult subject, and that the argument between them happened in the pages of scientific journals, Aitchison nevertheless seems to bring the two men together, making each the representative of a certain point of view. She then conducts an extraordinarily witty and engaging summary of a dispute between two different schools of thought. The whole thing takes just a few pages, but it is brilliantly done, with Aitchison introducing each new twist in the argument in such a way that you feel that it cannot possibly be answered by its opponent.

As she summarizes and quotes each position in turn, what could have been a dry and difficult subject comes to life – it becomes almost a duel. This is because Aitchison has put people into it, and has told a story about them. The argument is about whether language is learned by trial and error, punishment and reward, or whether there is something instinctive in our acquisition of it. Aitchison ends the debate by pointing out that the evidence shows that parents tend to reward their children for saying things that are true, rather than things that are grammatically correct. I laughed at the way she summarized it: 'If approval and disapproval worked in the way Skinner suggests, you would expect children to grow up telling the truth, but speaking ungrammatically. In fact the opposite seems to happen.'

Other books that manage to pull off the same kind of trick – taking complex material and bringing it to life, making it accessible – include Steven Pinker's *How the Mind Works*, Stephen Landsburg's *The Armchair Economist* and Bill Bryson's *A Short History of Nearly Everything*. You don't have to buy books though – if you're in the office just nip round the corner and buy a copy of the *Financial Times* newspaper or *The Economist* magazine. Both of these publications are extremely well written and thoroughly edited. Look for a good feature article (news stories are not usually so well written) and get that voice of calm authority in your mind.

All these different writers and publications are obeying the same rules. They are rules about simplicity, directness and courtesy to your reader – taking the time to explain and making sure that there is nothing that could cause confusion. It is the ways in which people apply these rules that reflects their individuality. The rules, far from constraining people, liberate them to be themselves.

Having good writing close at hand also provides you with an instant reference library. You can skim through it to check spellings, like a dictionary, to find alternative words, like a thesaurus, to see how it deals with capitals or acronyms, like a style guide, or you can look at how the author constructs sentences.

Summary

- Discover your characteristics as a writer:
  - Make a list of your strengths and weaknesses, and the words you overuse.
  - Use the questions at the beginning of the chapter to help you.
- Learn to vary your reading speed:
  - Reading speeds and styles differ from person to person.
  - Varying your reading speed allows you to understand how other people will read your writing.
  - If you habitually skim, then learning to slow down will help you to structure your points and tell a story.
  - If you read very slowly, then learning to speed up will help you to move at the same pace as your readers – as well as being a valuable skill in itself.
- Improve your writing by reading:
  - Read good non-fiction.
  - Read something well-written just before you write – it will help to remind you of the unwritten rules that underlie the pact between readers and writers.

2
Your Readers

The most important message in this book is: 'Write for the benefit of the people who will actually read your document.' Pretty much all of the other disciplines in writing follow on from this idea.

It sounds obvious. After all, who on earth *would* you write for if not your reader? But the fact is that most people who write at work make their most serious mistakes because they haven't thought about who will read the particular piece of writing they're working on. Writing is quite a personal activity: the act of setting your thoughts down in words on a page can really only be done alone – even if you are contributing to a project which has many authors. Alone with the page, people tend to re-fight old battles. As they write, they're thinking of a childhood teacher, probably long since retired, or a university professor, or their first boss, or the person who didn't like their last report.

It is also very easy to write with no reader in mind, to pour words into the void, to follow blindly the standard patterns, reuse the same old paragraphs and structures simply because that's how things are done.

Finally, you can go wrong by writing too much for yourself. As I'll say later, it's healthy to imagine yourself as the reader, but you have to consider – rigorously – how you differ from those you seek to communicate with. It is very easy to assume that, because you make the connection between two ideas, your audience will too, or to think that your knowledge, attitudes and assumptions are universally shared.

Reader profiling

To avoid these problems and to hit your real audience squarely between the eyes takes some thought and discipline. The way this is done by advertisers, marketers and the film and TV industries is to build up a profile of the desired audience which includes all the relevant information you can discover about them. The police use the same techniques for hunting criminals. Before you can discover anything else about them, you need to find out or decide who your readers are. The two basic questions you need to ask to discover and prioritize your different audiences are:

• What do readers want from this document?

Any group of readers who want the same sorts of things from the document constitutes an audience.
  You then need to ask:

• How important are those readers to you?

Mass vs individual audiences

One of the factors that most strongly influences your approach is whether your audience is an individual – or a few individuals – whom you could meet and find out extremely detailed information about. If the audience is too big for it to be practical for you to meet each person in it, or to talk to someone who has, then it is a mass audience. When writing for a mass audience, it is best to think of one or more individuals who are representative of the whole. In a way, mass audiences are more forgiving than individual audiences because they don't expect you to know anything about them as individuals. They won't, to put it basically, mind if you forget their birthdays.

It is possible for an audience to contain both mass and individual elements. For example, in writing this book I'm thinking of a mass audience, which I can guess at but never know, and an individual audience – the publisher – whom I have met and whose preferences and attitudes we've discussed in some detail. To be successful, I have to please both these audiences: one to put the books on the shelves and the other to take them off again.

How many different points of view do you have to cater for?

Audiences usually contain several different segments, and the better you can identify them and their preferences, the more successful your writing will be. For practical reasons, you won't want to identify more than two or three different audiences. You break an audience down by its agendas – or what it wants.

Sometimes many people can share a single agenda. When you make a proposal to a large corporation, for example, they might have published criteria which all the decision-makers will have to stick to and to use to justify their choice of supplier. If the decision-makers were all from the same country, with similar professional backgrounds and expectations, then you would have, in effect, a single audience. On the other hand, you might have a relatively small audience that has more than one agenda.

For example, I recently helped a company of auditors to write a proposal for work with an international corporation. The audience consisted of four people – three in the UK who represented the corporation's worldwide management, and one in the US, where the work was to be carried out. The UK audience was very sympathetic to the company I was working with, but the man in the US was sceptical. Their agendas coincided on many points – the most important of which was that they wanted a good job done and they didn't mind paying for it. Where they diverged was on the issue of control. One of the reasons the global management wanted to appoint my client was because my client worked for them in other countries and had good relations with their management – appointing my client would give the corporation's global management more control. The man in the US, on the other hand, was very keen to preserve as much autonomy as possible. I reasoned that we would have to make quite a mess of the proposal to put the UK management off my client. And as they didn't want to impose anything on the US, it made sense to focus on the man in that country. The tack we took was subtly to emphasize that we would always try to resolve problems and make decisions at the most local level possible, and that our reports to management would never include anything that hadn't already been discussed with the US.

False audiences

Where the apparent audience is different from the actual audience, I call the apparent audience a false audience. A false audience is one which, though outwardly important, is actually just a distraction. In the previous example, the decision-makers in London were more or less a false audience, because they had said they wouldn't impose anything on the US against its wishes. It was important not to fall into the trap of writing the proposal for the audience that was already sold on us, at the expense of the one we needed to convince.

False audiences are very common: the committee that ostensibly makes the decision actually rubber-stamps whatever the chairman says, or the report published for the rank and file employees is read only by managers – there are endless scenarios. You usually need to keep up the pretence of addressing the false audience, but you need to design your message for the actual audience.

Prioritizing audiences

False audiences obviously need to be accorded a very low priority, but if you have multiple audiences, you need to know which is the most important. If the various constituencies to which you're trying to appeal are genuinely equally important to you, then it is important to be clear about that too.

Filling in the reader profile

Write down each of your audiences and give each a descriptive name that distinguishes it from the others. Examples are *UK* and *US*, *managers* and *salespeople*, or *doctors*, *nurses* and *managers*. Prioritize them, say whether they are individual or mass audiences and note down if any of them are false audiences. Keep the number as small as possible – divide them only if their attitudes and priorities will lead them to differ significantly in the way they respond to what you say. For each audience, fill in the reader profile:

1. What unites this audience?
   Age? Tastes? Attitudes? Background? Aims?

2. How are they different from or similar to you?
   Industry? Company? Education? Nationality? Think also about the variety of English they speak and whether it is their first language.

3. What things do you deal with every day that your audience doesn't?
   Different divisions of your company? Different brand names? Background knowledge? Technical knowledge?

4. Why would they read this?
   Idly browsing? Interest in the subject? Personal gain? Obligation? Part of their job?

5. Do you know them personally?

6. Do they know more or less about the subject than you?

Some of this might not seem relevant, and it's true that not all of it will be. The important thing is that it gets you thinking about the people who will be reading your writing, and how they differ from you. Often, it will be relevant – if you're writing for a teenage audience in the UK, you can take it for granted that they will all be familiar with sending text messages on their mobile phones. If I were writing this book solely for that audience, I would just have written *texting* rather than *sending text messages on their mobile phones*.

Personas

Writing for a mass audience is difficult because we tend to dehumanize crowds. To humanize them, and make your job easier, it is a good idea to imagine one or two representative members of the audience. This can make an enormous difference. I use the term *personas* because it helps me to remember that these aren't real people, but only approximations – you can't rely on them.

The other reason is that the term is used in the software industry, where it has helped software designers to move away from the idea of trying to cram as many features as possible into each piece of software and towards looking at how people actually work and what they need to do most often and most easily. Use personas to help you imagine someone actually sitting down and reading your work. The idea of personas in software was pioneered by Alan Cooper in his book *The Inmates Are Running the Asylum*. There he advocates generating personas by conducting interviews with users (usually around 20 one-hour-long interviews), deciding on the users' goals, looking at what they do, what frustrates them and what pleases them, and then rating them on a list of around 20 variables (such as IT-literacy). Clusters of goals, motivations and variables are then looked for and used to construct two to seven personas.

I'm not suggesting that you go this far (unless you're working on a huge project), but it's important to remember the emphasis on usability, specificity and where the person will actually be.

The situation

This brings us to the importance of knowing not just who your readers are, but where they will be reading your writing, what they will be doing, why they will be reading it, what preconceptions they will have and, if possible, how they will be feeling. These might sound like impossible questions to answer, and sometimes they are, but often it is surprisingly easy to answer them.

For example, if you're sending an unsolicited sales letter (which will often have a multiple audience: the addressee and her secretary), it is a pretty safe bet that it will be read, if at all, at a desk in an office. Time is likely to be short, and attention divided; the reader has no obligation to read the whole thing and is likely to feel impatient or hostile towards it. It is likely to be competing with a lot of similar letters for attention. Clearly this rules out a long, detailed letter that is couched in legal language (unless you're trying to disguise the fact that it's a sales letter). Without much thought, we've come to some quite specific conclusions that will shape our approach.

This discipline is easy to work through, but a surprising number of people come to grief by ignoring it. You might assume that your audience will sit down quietly, well rested and with full concentration, and will read every word that you write, thinking hard about what you mean. In fact, for most things that you write, the exact opposite is true, and this has important consequences for the way we approach writing.

To use this book as an example again, I can imagine that if you go to the trouble of buying it, you will probably want to sit down and read at least part of it straight through. That is one reason for starting with the 'About You' section: it's a chance to get people comfortable with the book by reading and thinking about themselves. But for the book to be useful in the longer term, readers will need to be able to refer to specific information in a hurry – hence the summaries.

What to do with the reader profile

Having gone to all this trouble to think about who your audiences are, what they want and how they'll approach your writing, what do you do with the resulting information? Some books encourage you to imagine that you are your reader, but I think that this is too hard. What's more, research done by John R. Hayes of Carnegie Mellon University, Pennsylvania, suggests that most successful writers don't really do this. It's much easier to write for yourself, but imagining how you would feel if the description we have built up applied to you, if you were in the situation your readers will be in. You might not know how other people feel when they're stressed and distracted, but you certainly know how you feel then. This might seem like a subtle distinction, but I believe it makes a big difference.

One of the most common, and difficult, multiple audiences people face is when they're writing to a customer (for example, or another member of the public), but with the knowledge that their boss checks everything. This means that they're writing to please both the customer and their boss. This often makes people demoralized and affects the way they write – and it gets worse the more senior the boss is. If you ask these people to imagine being their boss, they usually can't – either because the resentment is too great or because they would feel presumptuous. But if you ask them to imagine themselves in their boss's situation, under the same constraints as him, they find it much easier. Approaching it this way tends to make people's assumptions much more reasonable – and it can help them to challenge their boss's changes if they don't understand them.

Summary

- Write for the benefit of the people who will actually read your document.
- Identify different audiences by asking:
  - What do readers want from this document?
  - How important are those readers to you?
- For each audience, ask:
  - What unites this audience?
  - How are they different from or similar to you?
  - What things do you deal with every day that your audience doesn't?
  - Why would they read this?
  - Do you know them personally?
  - Do they know more or less about the subject than you?

3
Your Goal and Your Message

What do you want your reader to do?

Successful writing affects its readers; it makes them behave differently than they would have if they hadn't read it. Obviously you can't affect people in the right way unless you know what that way is. Your writing needs to have a goal, and that goal should be expressed in terms of its effect on the reader. The more explicit you can make that goal, the better.

The most important thing to consider is whether you want an action as a result of your writing, or whether you want something less tangible, such as a change of attitude. Obviously, it is much easier to judge the success of writing which requires an action. The usual sorts of action people require from writing at work are:

- Signing a contract
- Buying something
- Sending money
- Attending a meeting
- Replying

- Answering a question
- Selling something
- Doing some work

The more subtle goals include:

- Adopting a particular attitude
- Changing a belief
- Remembering some information
- Understanding something

Although these goals are more difficult to observe and measure, they too require action in their way. This can take just as much, if not more, effort on the reader's part. Here are the goals of some typical writing tasks:

Task	Audiences	Goals
What are you writing?	Who are you writing it for?	What do you want them to do?
Email	Your boss	Know that you are organizing a meeting
	Your colleagues	Attend the meeting
Letter	A potential client	Agree to a meeting (the sale comes later)
Report	Shareholders	Keep their shareholdings
	Staff	Keep working hard in their jobs
	The public	Keep buying your products
Proposal	Finance Director	Appoint your company
	Board of Directors	Feel important

Your goal dictates your message

Your message is a one-line summary of what you want people to take away after reading your document. In the case of the email above, the message is simply: *There will be a meeting on Friday to discuss x*. As long as *x* is relevant and you send the email to your colleagues with a copy to your manager, you have achieved both of your goals.

The message supplies the information that makes behaving in the way you want the logical course of action for your audience. For example, in the example above of a report – in this case, the company's annual report – one of our goals is to make shareholders keep their shares. How do we get them to do this? Well, it depends on circumstances. Shareholders usually keep their shares if they are earning money from them, or if they believe they will in the near future. If the company has done well, the message would simply be: *Your shares are performing well*. That is the basic message we want to give the shareholders; that is what we want them to learn from the report. If the company hasn't done so well, then the message might be: *There are good reasons for our lacklustre performance this year, and your shares will perform well next year*. The details don't matter at this stage – the idea is just to write down the essence of what you want to convey to your readers.

What do your readers want?

Your message depends on what your readers want. Imagine that you are selling a printing service to medium-sized businesses. You send a letter to the manager of a firm of accountants with the goal of setting up a meeting. You consider what might make the manager agree to see you: she will certainly be interested in reducing her costs, but she doesn't have much time. So your messages are:

Our service reduces our clients' printing bills by 30 per cent per year, on average.
In a 20-minute meeting, I will estimate how much it would save you.

As long as your letter clearly and prominently says these two things, there is a good chance she will agree to a meeting.

Managing multiple messages

Often, there will be more than one important message that a document needs to convey. Going back to our annual report, we have three audiences to satisfy, and three different goals to achieve. That means we have at least three messages to convey. The messages we give to our different audiences will influence each other. We want to tell our shareholders that their shares have performed well, making them a handsome return, but we don't want customers to feel that we are making excessive profits from them. Nor do we want employees to feel that they are being under-rewarded for their work. In the light of this, the messages to our three audiences might be:

Shareholders: Your shares have performed reasonably well.
Customers: Our prices are lower than our competitors'.
Employees: The new pay structure is working.

To balance things up, we have toned down the triumphalism to shareholders, concentrated on prices rather than profits for customers and demonstrated to employees that they are getting a fair deal on pay.

How to get your messages across

Ideally, everything in your document will support these messages. You need to keep a lookout for places where you can give the messages in their strongest and simplest form. These include:

The title

Making your main message your title is the ideal, if it is possible. One proposal I wrote was entitled simply 'Reassurance', because that was what the company I was working for could provide that its competitors couldn't: a safe pair of hands. It was exactly what the client was looking for.

The strapline

If the title is prescribed, then you can add a strapline (or subtitle) communicating one of your main messages. If the title has to be 'Acme 2005 Annual Report', then the strapline could be 'A good year for shareholders'.

The summary

People pay most attention to what they read first, so it pays to get all your important messages in at the beginning. A good way of doing this is in a summary. Even in something as short as a letter, it can be a good idea to informally summarize your main messages, backing them up with information later on in the letter.

The beginnings of sections or chapters

You need to break longer pieces of writing down into sections, which I'll talk about in the next chapter. If you can, break it down in such a way that each of your sections relates to one of your key messages.

Telling your readers what to do next

One important type of message in any document is the 'what to do next' message: *Call me on extension 4324 – I'm here till five* or *Sign the enclosed form and return it in the pre-paid envelope*. This often goes at the end of a document – especially if it is short, like a letter or an email. While the most important message might also be convincing the reader to do something – such as buy your product or accept your recommendation – the 'what to do next' message is much more specific, immediate and modest.

Summary

- Have a clear, written goal for each piece of writing you do.
- For each audience, ask:
  - What do you want them to do or think?
  - What would make them do or think that?
- Use this to make a list of between one and three messages for each audience.
- Your document must deliver these messages clearly and consistently – everything in the document must support these messages.

4
Structure

Structure is an essential ingredient of good writing, and it is extremely useful for you as well as your readers. A good strong structure will allow you to be sure that you have covered everything and it will save you from repeating yourself. For your reader, it makes clear the links between the different topics or pieces of information that you give them. A structure gives readers an overall map or plan, a way of making sense of and fitting together the more detailed bits of information. A good structure tells the reader why they are reading what they are reading. That is very reassuring; it allows your reader to relax and go along with your flow.

Good structures, like good writing in general, tend to develop rather than appearing fully formed. Some people like to jot down a structure – a rough order of points – before they begin to write. Others prefer to splurge – to put everything down on paper as quickly as possible – and then see what structure has naturally emerged. They then work with and improve that structure. However you arrive at your structure, you must have considered your readers, your goals and your messages first.

There are two basic things that any structure has to do:

- Deliver all your main messages.
- Link different topics and information in a natural way.

When you are free to decide what goes in your document – as in a sales letter – you should make sure that every piece of information you give supports or proves one of your messages. You can structure the document around the main messages. Often, however, you will be constrained to provide certain information whether you want to or not. In this case, devise a structure that presents the information as cleanly and clearly as possible for the reader, and add your messages where you can.

Linking

Linking points together naturally and coherently is one of the things people tend to find most difficult in writing. Once you know the different options for doing it, it can be quite fun to figure out coherent ways of presenting apparently unrelated information. There are four main ways of doing it:

- Find an overarching theme.
- Relate things in chronological order, as a narrative or story.
- Build an argument.

- Break things down into categories based on similarities and differences.

Find an overarching theme

In the example I gave in the last chapter, of the annual report that must please shareholders, employees and customers, the overarching theme might be responsibility. The company might say, as most do nowadays, that they have a responsibility to everyone with a stake in the company, including shareholders, employees and customers, and that it is their duty to balance these responsibilities. This provides a very good structure for presenting different kinds of information and messages to the different audiences.

Relate things in chronological order, as a narrative or story

This is not usually used as a structure for a whole document, because it can make it difficult to separate out different themes. No organization would present their annual report as a list of the things it had done that year, in chronological order. It is always better to summarize what it has achieved in the various different markets or areas in which it works. Documents that do use this structure include histories, journals and letters of complaint (and their replies), which often need to focus on precisely what happened and in what order. This structure emphasizes cause and effect, so it can help to justify actions by giving their context.

Build an argument

An argument or analysis can be a good way of linking
different messages or information. A report on the health
service, for example, might say: 'There are three funda-
mentals for an efficient health service: informed patients,
motivated staff and modern facilities.' These three
things could then form the three sections of the report.

*Break things down into categories based on their
similarities or differences*

A consumer organization, campaigning on various
different issues, presented its work issue by issue.
Although they hadn't deliberately confined their work
to specific areas, by looking for similarities in and
differences between the sorts of work they had done,
they managed to split it all into four areas: trading
fairly, food, basic services (such as water and energy)
and money matters.

Explain your structure

Not only do you need a rationale for the order in
which you introduce your material, but you have to
make sure that your readers know what it is. This can
be done very simply and economically. In a report,
you might simply say:

Our work this year has been concentrated in four different
areas: trading fairly, food, basic services (such as water and
energy) and money matters. This report takes each of these
areas in turn, explaining what we have achieved over the past
year and setting out our plans for the next.

In a letter, it could be even shorter. This sentence might go at the end of the first paragraph of a reply to a letter of complaint:

To make sure I address all your points, I will answer them in the order in which you raise them in your letter.

Summarizing and reordering

Some people prefer to write first and structure afterwards, which can work just as well as working out the structure in advance. The best way to do this is to summarize the points you have made, and then work out an order for them that means you address each topic once, and you can move naturally from one to the next.

Sometimes this can be done just by writing down the topic of each paragraph. I recently edited an article by a computer company that sells a technology allowing employees to access files on their employer's PC network, no matter where they are. With a technical subject like this, it is even more important than usual to be as clear and non-technical as possible. I began by noting down what was happening in each paragraph:

Paragraph	Topic
1	**Remote access** makes **computer security** more important.
2	Nowadays **employees** need **remote access** to do their jobs.

Paragraph	Topic
3	The **companies you work with** also need **remote access**. You could use an **extranet**, but they're expensive and time-consuming.
4	**Remote access** can compromise **security**.
5	**Companies you work with** shouldn't be given access to all of your data. You need to **encrypt** all information.
6	Without **remote access**, **employees** and **companies you work with** can't do their jobs.
7	**Virtual Private Networks (VPNs)** could be the answer. VPNs that use **IPSec** technology have lots of problems.
8	**Extranets** aren't a good idea. VPNs that use **SSL** technology are a good idea.
9	**SSL** VPNs solve all possible problems.
10	**SSL** VPNs **encrypt** all the information they send.
11	**Companies** need to open their **networks** and protect their **data** at the same time. SSL VPNs are the answer.

I've put the key terms – the article's cast of characters – in bold. From this, it's quite easy to see that each of the characters crops up several times: extranets are dismissed in the third paragraph and then again in the eighth; and the point about the necessity of remote access is made in the second and the sixth paragraphs.

It is possible to make the article much more comprehensible just by changing the running order, so that each point is dealt with only once, and each contributes to the overall message. The revised structure goes like this:

- Remote access is necessary for every company's employees.
- Non-employees (including other companies) also need selective access.
- There are dangers in remote access.
- It is worth overcoming the dangers.
- Traditional (IPSec) VPNs aren't the answer.
- Neither are extranets.
- SSL VPNs solve all the problems.

In this example, I have left the main message till the end, rather than putting it at the beginning as I usually would. That is because the technical term 'SSL VPN' wouldn't mean anything to the audience – company managers – without being explained. In order to get them to pay attention long enough for me to explain it, I describe a need with which they are likely to identify. By the end of the article, we have answered the need.

Summary

- There are two basic things that any structure has to do:
  - Deliver all your main messages.
  - Link different topics and information in a natural way.

- There are four main ways of structuring a piece of writing:
  - Find an overarching theme.
  - Relate things in chronological order, as a narrative or story.
  - Build an argument.
  - Break things down into categories based on similarities and differences.
- Remember to tell your readers what structure you are using, and how the different parts of your document are linked.
- You can develop your structure either before or after you write your first draft.
- To fix the structure of a piece of writing, list the topics covered in each paragraph and then arrange them so that each topic appears only once.

5
The Medium

One of the main factors that affects your structure is the medium you are using. Each has its own demands and conventions.

Letter

Letters follow a very prescribed format, consisting of a few defined elements.

Your name and address
Give your full name, title, company and address here, along with your telephone number if it will help. However, leave this space blank if you are writing on your company's headed paper: in which case their logo, address and main telephone numbers will appear in this position.

Their name, title and address
Give the name, job title and company of the person you are writing to. You should also give a form of their postal address here. You don't need to write the full

	Your name **1** Your address Your telephone number (optional)
Their name **2** Their job title Their company Their shortened address	
Date **3**	
Greeting **4**	
Message **7**	
Sign-off **4**	
Signature **5**	
Your name **6** Your title	

thing since that will be on the envelope (unless, of course, you're using window envelopes). To shorten their address, just give the first line (*12 Formby Gardens*, or *The Larches*) and the town.

Date
The convention in business is to give the date in the form *12 October 2004* – with no comma after the month and no *th* or *rd* after the day. If you want to say what day of the week it is, that goes first, followed by a comma: *Tuesday, 12 October 2004*.

Greeting and sign-off
This always begins *Dear*. For the full rules about how to address dukes, earls, ambassadors and high-ranking clergy, have a look at Debrett's Peerage. They have an online guide at http://www.debretts.co.uk/etiquette/correct_forms_of_address.html. Otherwise there are only three options:

- If you have no idea who will read your letter, begin *Dear Sir or Madam* and sign off with *Yours faithfully*.
- If you know the name of the person you are writing to, but are not intimate friends, write *Dear Mr Matthews* and sign off with *Yours sincerely*.
- If you're on first-name terms with someone, write *Dear Jim* and end *Yours, Best wishes* or *All the best*.
- The better you know someone, the less the conventions matter, and the more free you are to improvise.

If you have reasonable handwriting, it shows a more personal touch to write the greeting and sign-off by hand.

Signature

There's not much to say here, except to urge you to adopt a signature that bears some relation to your name. If you are signing the letter for someone else, such as a boss or colleague, the usual practice is to sign your own name and write *p.p.* next to theirs. However, because *p.p.* stands for 'per procurationem', Latin for 'through the agency of', it is better to put your signature *beneath* their name, with the letters p.p. to the left of your signature. That way, you can also write your own full name beneath your signature – which can be helpful for the recipient to know.

Your name and title

Give your full name, with your job title and company underneath.

The message

Letters are much easier to read if they are broken down into fairly short paragraphs, of perhaps two to five sentences each. Whatever kind of letter you're writing, the first and final paragraphs have specific functions.

First paragraph

The first paragraph is an introduction: it should say why you are writing. If you are replying to a letter of theirs, you need to make that clear. You can say, *Thank you for your letter of 15 November*, but anything that links your letter to theirs is fine. If you aren't replying to a letter of theirs, you usually need to begin by introducing yourself – by saying where you met or how you heard about them, or by mentioning people you both know. Although the first paragraph is usually no more than four sentences long, it is best to give your main message here if you can fit it in. You can then expand on it, explain it and provide supporting information in the rest of the letter. If it won't fit in the first paragraph, then put it right at the beginning of the second paragraph.

Final paragraph

The final paragraph wraps the letter up. It usually repeats the overriding sentiment expressed in the letter – thanks, apology, welcome – and expresses a positive wish – *I wish you the best of luck in your new job* or *I hope I have explained things clearly enough*. It then gives options for getting in touch: *If you have any questions, please call me on [number]*.

These two paragraphs help give the letter its shape. The first tells you straight away who is writing to you and why, leading naturally into the main body of the letter. And the last tells you that, having made his point, set out his complaint or offered his services, the writer wishes you well and can be contacted easily.

Tone

People tend to be too formal in letters, using expressions like *I am now in receipt of your correspondence of Thursday last*, *I trust this meets with your requirements*, or *It was noted following a review that the invoice remained unpaid*. Watch out for anything that could sound patronizing or impersonal. There are polite, human-sounding ways of saying anything: *I have received the letter you sent on Thursday, I hope this is convenient* or *You haven't yet paid the invoice.*

Email

```
[Greeting]

[Ice-breaker]
[Main message]
[Other messages or supporting information]
[Explanation of attachments]
[Whether you want a reply]

[Sign-off]

[Your name]
_____

[Your name]
[Your address]
[Your telephone number]
[Your mobile number]
[Your email address]
_____
```

Emails are useful for sending short, simple messages, documents and for asking questions. Like letters, emails can also be broken down into separate elements. Although emails may seem very free-form, there are more conventions to them than you might think.

To line

In general, only include people in the to line if you want a reply from them.

Cc line

In general, include people in the cc line if they need to know everything in the email but do not need to react to it. If only one part of the email applies to them, then forward the email to them with a note saying what they need to read, why, and what action they should take.

Bcc line

Only rarely use this. Addresses here are kept hidden. It is useful for circulars and newsletters, where you don't want to compromise people's privacy by broadcasting their email address to all the other recipients.

Subject line

Try to make the subject line do as much work as possible. To make it really useful, put the whole message in the subject line: *Meeting with ACME postponed to 3 p.m.* or *Please call John Acton.*

Make sure you use the subject line for your reader's benefit, not for yours. If you send an email to me, *Clarity* might seem the obvious subject line, but it won't help me to know whether it's worth reading. Think of the subject line as an advert for the email.

Greetings and sign-offs

Always use a greeting before the main body of the email and a sign-off afterwards, followed by your name. When replying, take your cue from the person who sent the email: use the same greeting and sign-off as them unless you think it is inappropriately familiar or formal.

Write *Hello John* and *Best wishes*, *Regards* or *Thanks* for most everyday purposes, including business emails. Write *Dear Mr Green* and *Regards* for very formal emails, or if it doesn't feel right to use the recipient's first name – as with an angry customer or someone much further up the hierarchy than you.

Ice-breakers

Emails always read much more coldly than you would expect. For this reason, you need to make sure you always say something warm to counteract the inherent coolness of the medium. This should usually be the first or the last sentence of the message – or sometimes both. Something simple will do.

At the beginning you can write something like *It was good to see you on Tuesday* or *Thanks for your help this morning*. At the end you might say *Looking forward to seeing you soon* or *Please give me a ring if you want a hand*. The final ice-breaker can be given a paragraph of its own, either before the sign-off or instead of it.

Attachments

If you include attachments, make sure you say in the message what they are. If there is more than one, quote the filenames, particularly if the filenames aren't self-explanatory.

Signature

Include a signature that has your contact details. Put a blank line (or a solid line of underscores – by pressing the Shift and Minus keys) before and after your signature. Some email programmes add the signature after the message has been sent, which means you can end up with the message running into the signature.

Signatures usually include your full name, your job title, your company, your postal address (optional), your direct-line telephone number or your mobile number, your company's reception number (optional) and your web address (optional).

Other conventions

Make it clear whether you want a reply. If not, put *FYI* (for your information) in the subject line.

Try not to address more than one subject in a single email.

Because emails are so like conversation, people tend to forget that their tone of voice might not come across. Jokes, sarcasm and implied meanings will tend not to work unless you know the recipient well.

Break things up with plenty of white space. Put different topics, questions or whatever on different lines, and always give web or email addresses a line to themselves.

Remember they aren't text messages: spell everything out in full (rather than saying *c u l8r*) and use capitals and punctuation – it makes emails easier to read.

Reread it before sending. This should also stop you forgetting to send attachments. Do a spellcheck. On PCs this is usually done by pressing F7.

Many company email systems add a very long disclaimer to every message. To keep your email from running into this message, leave a couple of lines after your message.

Don't use a PS. They tend to get lost – in the disclaimer, the signature or previous message.

In emails, your goal is often very clear, and it usually dictates your subject line and the first paragraph of your message.

Report

Reports come in different shapes and sizes, depending on their purpose, but it is possible to construct a standard template that can be snipped and adjusted for most uses:

- Cover
- Contents page
- Foreword
- Executive summary
- Main body
- Glossary
- Appendices

Cover/title page

If the report is more than about three pages long, it is a good idea to have a cover. Even if it is just a piece of white paper with the title on it, a cover makes the report look more professional. The most important requirement of the title page is that it prominently displays the title, clearly and cleanly. Put it about a quarter or a third of the way down the page and use a relatively large, clear font, like Arial 48pt. Put your name, or the name of your company, about the same distance from the bottom of the page, in the same size font, or perhaps slightly smaller.

It is a good idea to have the cover professionally designed if you can – or to get a designer to do a standard template for all your company's reports, if you do a fair number of them. If you can't afford a designer, the main thing is to keep it all clean and simple. Use only one font and make sure there's plenty of blank space, and remember not to spoil the cover by putting a page number on it. You should also avoid putting words in block capitals – even in titles they are harder to read and look somehow bad-tempered. Underlining also makes words harder to read. If you use graphics, keep them simple, restrained and in line with margins and text. It is also important to make sure they are of a high enough resolution to be printed out. Some things can look fine on the screen but terrible in print, so be sure to test in advance.

Contents page

Contents
Foreword	2
Exec. summary	3
The problem	5
The solution	8

Contents pages are very useful for readers. They make it easier to get to the parts of the document in which the reader is most interested – which is why it is essential to use descriptive headings containing words and concepts with which the reader is familiar. No one pores over contents pages for hours, but a quick glance can give the reader a surprising amount of information about your report:

- How technical it is
- How reader-friendly it is
- How (and whether) it is organized
- Whether it covers a subject in which the reader is particularly interested

Explanatory section headings using terms that are familiar to the reader will reassure on the first two points. Incidentally, if you know your readers are familiar with technical or specialist terms, don't be shy of using them in your headings – it will show your readers that the document has been written with them in mind.

Grouping headings into sections can be very helpful for you and your readers. It gives readers a reassuring sense that there is some structure and method to the document, and it helps you to organize your thoughts. Be sure to check that the page numbers are correct before the document goes out – they often go wrong, even (or especially) if they have been inserted automatically by your word-processing software.

Foreword

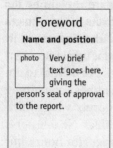

Foreword

Name and position

photo | Very brief text goes here, giving the person's seal of approval to the report.

A foreword is an endorsement, a seal of approval from someone in authority. This could be someone in your own organization, such as a chairman or senior partner, or some eminent person in a relevant field, such as a well-known spokesman or a respected authority. If your report is for people outside your own organization – the public or a client, for example – then you may well want it to begin with a foreword.

The purpose of the foreword is not to summarize what the report says, but to convince readers that it is worth taking seriously. This often means that it mentions the report's central message or recommendation, but in the context of introducing the author, praising the methodology or explaining the importance of the topic.

Executive summary

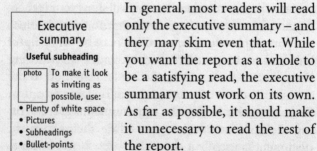

Executive summary

Useful subheading

photo | To make it look as inviting as possible, use:
• Plenty of white space
• Pictures
• Subheadings
• Bullet-points

In general, most readers will read only the executive summary – and they may skim even that. While you want the report as a whole to be a satisfying read, the executive summary must work on its own. As far as possible, it should make it unnecessary to read the rest of the report.

An executive summary is simply

a summary. I have no idea how the 'executive' got in there – perhaps it is a remnant of the eighties fad for making everything 'executive', from washrooms to assistants. Whatever the reason, the term is universally used. The idea is that a busy executive should be able to read this summary and know:

• What the report covers
• What its conclusions or recommendations are

The secret of executive summaries is to cut to the chase: give your readers the concluding sentence of the report right up front. Don't worry that you are somehow 'spoiling the suspense' of the report. Oddly enough, the more you spoil the suspense, the more likely people are to read the rest of the report.

Think of the executive summary as an ambassador for the report: putting its case and presenting it in its most attractive aspect. If there is anything in the report that you want people to know about, put it in the executive summary. And if there is one key message that you want to deliver, make it the first sentence of the executive summary.

Subheadings and layout can help a lot to make an executive summary more inviting and accessible. Keep the paragraphs short, break them up with white space and add a couple of relevant graphics, if you have them.

Try to keep the executive summary down to one or two pages, or it will need a summary of its own. Writing the summary before you tackle the rest of the document is usually a good idea – it will force you to crystallize your ideas and set down your main messages.

It can then act as a plan and summary, helping you to write the rest of the report. At the end, you will inevitably want to revise or rewrite it, but it will have helped you get your ideas down in the meantime.

At the end of your executive summary, tell readers how the document is structured – it will help them feel that they know where they are with the document, and it will help you to spot any weaknesses in its organization.

Main body

The main body of a report is where you present information, set out arguments and fill in the blanks. It fulfils the promise of the executive summary, presenting everything the reader needs to know to accept your message. Chapter 4 discussed ways of structuring material, all of which apply equally to reports. In addition, it is important to remember that each section or chapter of a report should make sense on its own, and that each should address a particular area of interest or a particular group of readers.

For example, if you were writing a report on the oil industry for international investors, it might make sense to take a chapter for each of the main countries or markets, so the investors can choose where to put their money. Or if you were writing a report to advise a company's management about IT strategy, you might split it into three options or scenarios, and give each of them its own chapter. That would be more relevant for decision-makers than using each chapter to explain a different kind of technology, for example.

Glossary

> **Glossary**
>
> **Term**
> Brief definition.
>
> **Term**
> Brief definition.
>
> **Term**
> Brief definition.

If you've used any technical terms, put them in a glossary after the main body of your report. A glossary can be helpful even if your audience is as technically literate as you are, because technical terms can often be used in more than one way, and it can be helpful for your readers to know which definition you are using. List terms in alphabetical order.

Appendices

> **Appendix I:**
> **Description**
>
> Raw data or detailed information. This is often given in tables.

Appendices are for detailed material or raw data that might be useful for some of your readers but which would just get in the way for most. Appendices are usually given Roman numerals (I, II, III, IV, V, etc.), but it helps to give them a descriptive title too, e.g. *Appendix I: UK management survey results.*

Proposal

Proposals follow exactly the same structure as reports, but with a few modifications and additions:

- Covering letter
- Cover

- Contents page
- Needs and responses
- Your questions answered
- The team
- Main body
- Fees
- Glossary
- Appendices

There are also a few general points to bear in mind.

The tone

You need to be as specific as possible in your document and say what you will actually do, rather than talking in generalities. If, for example, you're submitting a proposal to provide tax advice, try not to say, *Tax is a complex area, requiring a detailed knowledge of the relevant regulations*, which is a truism – not to be argued with, but not very helpful either. Instead, try to say things like, *On the day after we are appointed, Mike Biggs will begin an audit of your tax submissions for the last year*. It might not sound so sonorous or high-falutin, but it contains a specific action which will benefit the client, rather than just words. In the same vein, write about what you *will* do, not about what you *would* do *should* you be appointed. Using *will* is a powerful suggestion to buy: it looks confident, and it's much easier to read and write.

Taking your cue from the client

When companies want others to tender for a piece of work, they often issue a request for proposals (RFP) or an invitation to tender (ITT) – interchangeable terms for documents which describe what the company wants doing. I use the term RFP, because it's a more distinctive abbreviation. Usually, the proposal should be based on the RFP, following its structure and basing the main messages on its most important requirements.

However, sometimes RFPs are not very good. They tend to suffer from the same sorts of problems as proposals: being too generic, having been adapted from a standard template, being difficult to follow, being poorly organized and missing crucial points of detail. If there is an RFP, use discussions with your client to supplement your understanding of what they want. If the RFP is not an accurate reflection of their needs, then feel free to use a different structure. If you do this, you need to show how your proposal relates to the structure of their RFP. The best way to do that is to have a page near the beginning of your document – usually just after the executive summary – called 'Your questions answered', which shows where in your document you respond to each part of the RFP.

Playing to your strengths

Inevitably, some of your client's needs will be very generic and any of your competitors will be able to satisfy them as easily as you can. Before you begin writing the proposal, discuss with colleagues what you

think your various competitors' strategies will be and
write a summary of each. Then focus the document
on the areas in which you are strongest – for example,
price or experience. Showing that your strengths match
your client's needs requires building an argument. This
is the most important and usually the most overlooked
part of a proposal.

To devise your argument, put yourself in your
client's shoes and ask yourself how you would make
your decision: what are your criteria, your prejudices,
your experiences and your needs? Create an argument
that answers all of these in a way that plays to your
own company's strengths. For example, one of our
clients was the auditor for a subsidiary of a multinational corporation. Although the subsidiary was very
happy with our client's services, when the contract
came up for renewal it was the multinational's management who had to decide whether to continue with our
client. The problem was that the rest of the multinational was audited by our client's main competitor,
so all other things being equal it made sense for the
subsidiary to be audited by the competitor as well. The
core of the proposal we produced was that all other
things were far from equal – it was a critical time for
the subsidiary, and what it needed was continuity and
a deep understanding of its business, rather than a
disruptive change of auditors.

Covering letter

Most proposals are accompanied by a covering letter
that fulfils much the same purpose as a foreword. This

usually means the most senior person involved in or responsible for the project writing to:

- Commend the team
- State the key message

Here is an example of a covering letter for a proposal:

> Dear Mr Marques,
>
> Garcia International is already one of our best clients in the mining industry, and the opportunity to act as your engineering consultants marks a significant development in our relationship with you.
>
> In this relationship, our technical director Bob Adamson's detailed knowledge of your engineering division will be extremely valuable. I have also worked closely with Michel Beauvais over the last few weeks, and, having met the engineering team he will lead, I am confident that you will receive excellent service at all times.
>
> I will personally ensure that Michel Beauvais and Bob Adamson have all the support and resources they need to do exactly what they set out in this proposal.
>
> Yours sincerely,
>
> Marshal Anderson

It is becoming usual for the covering letter to be bound into the proposal itself. If you do this, put it immediately after the cover.

Executive summary – or needs and responses

As with a report, an executive summary is essential. This is often given as a table enumerating your client's needs, setting out your response to each of those needs, and then saying how they will benefit from that. Make sure that the things you write in the 'Needs' column really do reflect their needs. Find this out from conversations with the client, from discussions among yourselves and from a careful reading of the RFP. You also need an introductory paragraph:

We have designed this proposal to answer your most important questions as quickly as possible. You need to know that we will make a smooth transition, stick to your timetable and put our best people on the job – all within a three-year fixed fee, and all supported by clear and open communication.

Needs	Responses
Your tax information needs to get to investors on time.	We will turn paperwork around within ten days.
You need us to stick to your timetable – especially in February and March.	We have already ensured that every member of our team has the time available in February and March.

The team

The people who will carry the work out and be in day-to-day contact with the client are usually a big factor in the client's decision. For this reason, it is always best to give brief biographies of the main three to six people (never more than ten – others can go in

> **Michael Finch**
>
> Team leader
>
> | | |
> |---|---|
> | photo | Michael will be co-ordinating our team to make sure we have the right people at each of your sites. He has been a senior |
>
> partner with us for seven years, working with other clients in your industry, including AcmeCars and GoodLorries.
>
> Referee
> Gerald Mann
> CEO, AcmeCars
> 01123 233 4122
>
> (For full CV, see appendix)

the appendix) early on in the document. Set down relevant or impressive experience or achievements for each. If you can, give the name and telephone number of a client referee for each of them, so that your prospective client can find out what it's like to work with them.

Some companies like to give a quote from each person, or have everyone write their own biographies in the first person. However, I think it's best not to do this because it makes them uneven (especially in length) and it means that you end up with too many weak jokes and unconvincing claims of being excited at the prospect of working with the client. It is much better to have one person writing all the biographies. It means you can get them to a standard length and format, and have an objective view of what will be relevant, interesting and impressive to that client.

Try to include pictures: it makes the team seem like people, and it will help your client to recognize them when they turn up to pitch in person.

Main body

The advice I gave in Chapter 4 applies here, as does the advice about how to organize the main body of a report. The only additional thing to mention about proposals is that you have to take extra care to structure chapters and sections according to your readers' needs and the way their company is organized.

The temptation is to structure your proposal around your products or your company's divisions. Resist the temptation: the names of your company's products and divisions are jargon to everyone else. If, for example, your company is split into an oil division and a gas division, you might be tempted to have a chapter on oil and a chapter on gas. But if your prospective client is organized on geographic grounds, with a Europe division and an Asia division, then you should make those your chapter headings because there will be people in your audience who are interested in one but not the other.

Fees

Don't try to hide your fees. Put them fairly close to the front of the document, not in an appendix, and call that section 'Fees' rather than some euphemism like 'Remuneration'. As well as being polite and considerate to your reader, this makes you look confident.

Remember to break them down in whatever way the client has specified and to label each element clearly.

Appendices

Because there is always a temptation to supply unnecessary information in proposals (just in case it makes a difference), appendices are very useful. Use them to separate out supporting information (which might be useful for specialists) from the main messages. Here's an example showing which material should go in the main section and which in the appendices.

Subject	Main document	Appendices
The team	Brief biographies of the main people.	Full CVs for the whole team.
Fees	Fees, fee structure, options.	Detailed calculations, full assumptions, costings.
IT	The name of the IT system, the benefits for this particular client.	Background information about how it works, licensing, who has access to what, etc.

If appendices get too large, you can sometimes supply them as a separate document. However, ask your client before you do this. If things have got to this stage, then you are almost certainly putting too much in the appendices. Remember that the client doesn't need every piece of information in advance, just the bits that will help them to make a decision. Information overload can make that decision more difficult.

Article or press release

If you write an article as part of your job, it is likely to be for an internal publication like a newsletter, or for promotional purposes. In either case, the most important thing is to think about how it might be relevant to your readers: how could what you have to say benefit them?

The running order for an article goes like this:

- Hook
- Statement of message
- Discussion
- Conclusion / restating the message

You should begin with a hook to get them interested: a question, a provocative fact or a description of a problem which your readers share. Then move on to state your message. Sometimes the message and the hook are given together in a short introductory paragraph printed in bold or otherwise set apart from the main text. This kind of paragraph is called a standfirst.

Think carefully about what your message is. State it in the first paragraph, so people know what they're going to read about, and then restate it in a modified form at the end. This might mean phrasing it as a question at the beginning and a statement at the end:

How can pensioners save money on their winter heating bills? . . . Switching to Acmegas cut pensioners' fuel bills by 20 per cent on average.

Use quotes to bring in other points of view, state tricky opinions or reinforce your points:

Not everyone is happy with the new approach. 'This kind of commercialism is damaging the community,' says Marilyn Aitchison of the Community Volunteer Association.

Use quotes, facts or statistics to back up your points so that you avoid making unsubstantiated assertions. Numbers can be particularly useful. As my colleague Richard Heller says in his book *High Impact Speeches*, numbers are metaphors. They can be used to illustrate points, but you have to tell people what they mean and put them into context.

Explain anything that you cannot guarantee the reader will be familiar with. Whenever a new person, product, company, abbreviation – or anything else with a name – appears in your article, add a quick description:

Gail Ponders, our chief financial officer, believes that . . .

. . . using RFID tags – microchips that are replacing barcodes as a way of keeping track of stock.

I think of these things as being like the characters in a play or novel. You need to keep their number manageable or people will be overwhelmed by the amount of new things they have to remember. As a rule of thumb, I'd say it is best not to have more than ten in a thousand words.

Brochure

The most important thing in brochures is to get the basics right and to check everything thoroughly: people are expected to make decisions on the basis of what they read in the brochure. Try to restrain yourself from grandiloquence. I once edited a brochure that contained nonsensical phrases like, *This elegant white ballroom fashions a stylish opulence and provides a feeling of pomp grandeur making it ideal for obtaining distinctive photographic images.* This leaves readers with a number of questions: how do you fashion an opulence? What does pomp grandeur feel like? Is obtaining distinctive photographic images like taking photos? Instead, think about the sort of information your customers are likely to need and give it to them clearly and thoroughly, in a friendly way.

When writing brochures it is especially important to think about those things that are so close that you cannot see them: what industry you're in, what you do and what benefits your products provide. These can give you the basis for a descriptive strapline – such as *Family holidays in France* – that will help make your brochure more useful. As in all selling, you need to concentrate on benefits rather than features. The only exception is when the audience is very expert and knows what the features mean – as with some kinds of IT products.

You also need to give readers a means of getting in touch with you – give all your contact information, and say which means of communication you prefer. You could also consider offering an incentive for getting in touch, such as a free gift, a voucher or an introductory offer. All of this needs to be in a very visible place, such as the front or back cover.

Finally, try to keep it short – you don't want to overwhelm people. About ten pages is usually the maximum.

Front cover

```
Company Name


        graphic
        /logo



        Strapline
```

Inside page 1

```
        Strapline
      Introductory text
       setting out the
       main benefits.

        Product 1
       Benefits and
       description.

        Product 2
       Benefits and
       description.
```

Inside page 2

```
        Inducement
     Details of introductory
          offer, etc.


        How to get
         in touch
       Contact details.
```

Back cover

```
      Company Name

       • Bullet points
       • Main benefits
       • Big messages

        Contact details.
```

Leaflet

Leaflets are rather like very concentrated versions of brochures. If they are printed on just one side, then they can contain only one message, which must be carefully tailored for the situation in which they will be distributed and for the people who will take them. It is usually important not to try to say too much. Very often you will want your audience to have some questions so that they can get in touch with you to ask them. Again, it is very important to give people the means and the inducement to get in touch. The three things you need are:

- Attention grabber – a graphic, a tease or an offer that you can't help but see when you pick up the leaflet
- Company name
- Contact details

Webpage

Because of the way people browse the Internet, moving quickly from site to site and page to page, you need to make sure that each webpage deals with only one subject (apart from the front page). Each one also needs to be as short as possible, since most people don't like reading large blocks of text on their monitors. It is also important to keep the layout simple and clean, with plenty of white space – this avoids things getting lost, and it means that your readers are less likely to suffer if they have an older web-browser or a smaller monitor than others. Keeping it short, simple and clean also reduces loading times for people with slower connections.

All writing depends on people knowing where they are within the structure, and websites are no exception. Each page should have a link to important parts of the overall structure – such as the introduction, the home page and frequently asked questions (FAQs). It is important to keep things consistent. One website I reviewed recently completely confused me, because pages had different titles in different menus. For example, on the home page there was a link to the rather dull-sounding 'facts and figures', which turned into the far more inviting 'offbeat facts' when the page appeared.

CV

There are all sorts of different ways of laying out CVs, but as with most writing, the thing that underlies them all is the principle of helping your reader. With CVs, this means making your name the most prominent thing on the page, more prominent than 'Curriculum Vitae'. There's nothing worse for recruiters and interviewers than going through a big pile of documents entitled 'Curriculum Vitae' on which they have to search for the candidate's name. The reader knows it's a CV, the thing that identifies it is your name. In addition, a small photo can help to humanize you, turning you from a piece of paper into a person.

It is best to limit your CV to a single piece of paper, and to give only the information that the reader will find most helpful. Put the basics down first, giving contact details, including a phone number that is easy to spot, along with your date of birth and marital status. Then list your most recent and relevant qualifications. After that give your employment highlights: your last job and the most relevant and impressive ones before that, with a brief description of the most relevant and impressive things that you did in each. In fact, *relevant* and *impressive* are the key words to keep in mind when writing a CV.

It is also a good idea to give hobbies and interests, and your aspirations for the future. Then give the names and contact details of your referees – as well as how you know them. Some people recommend giving yourself a strapline – a very brief description of yourself that functions as the message you want your CV to convey, such as 'experienced writer and editor'. If you feel comfortable doing this and if it might genuinely help the reader to understand what sort of person you are and why they should employ you, then it's probably a good idea. If, on the other hand, the idea makes you cringe, I would give it a miss.

6

The Way You Work

One of the benefits of writing at work is that you rarely have to do it entirely on your own. Even if your writing doesn't have to be formally checked or approved by anyone, it is likely that other people will be involved in deciding what you write. The next chapter explains how to manage the process of writing as teamwork. This chapter is about writing on your own.

If you aren't part of a team, it is as well to act as much as possible as though you were. It is easy to get too close to any piece of writing, so getting a second opinion always helps. This might just mean talking something over with a friend, but if you can, get some-one to read what you've written. Even if they aren't great writers, other people often give you insights you hadn't expected. Apart from anything else they are good guinea pigs – if they find something difficult to understand then your real readers probably will too.

Writing in teams works best when everyone knows their roles, and, curiously enough, the same principle applies even when you're working entirely alone. You need to divide up the tasks and approach each as though you were a different person. Imagine yourself as a one-man newspaper, taking on each role in turn. Every article in a newspaper goes through a whole chain of people: commissioning editor, researcher, writer and subeditor. The editor knows the readership and decides what subjects will appeal to them. He commissions the article, the researcher gets background information, and the writer writes it. The editor checks to see whether it is what he wanted, and the article might go through a couple of drafts before it fits the bill. Then the editor hands it over to a subeditor, who polishes it and corrects grammatical or spelling errors.

You need to become each of these people. To avoid problems, you need to keep these activities separate, and to approach each in a different frame of mind. Very often, you will find that most of the weaknesses you identified in Chapter 1 are associated with one particular type of activity. Here's how to work:

- When you are planning your document, be hard-headed, cynical and realistic – like a Fleet Street editor. Once the writing is finished, read it over again with this attitude to make sure that it does what you planned.

- When you are researching your document, make a list in advance of things that you will need to know. To avoid over-researching, stick only to those things. When the writing is finished, go back and check any claims or facts that you aren't sure of.

- When you are writing your document, don't worry about getting it right, just get it down – get anything down. Don't judge, censor or edit as you write.

- Leave subediting till the very end. When you're

subediting, look at the writing clinically, applying the rules of punctuation and grammar, and looking out for common mistakes.

Avoiding writer's block

Writing tends to go smoothly when people follow something like that process, becoming at different times the wily editor, the diligent researcher, the prolific writer and the meticulous subeditor. Problems tend to come about when people try to take on the wrong role at the wrong time:

1. The writer sits down to work without consulting the editor; he has no idea of why or to whom he is writing. He plucks empty phrases out of the air to fill up the space, and ends up saying nothing.

2. Instead of the writer, the researcher sits down to do the writing. She writes a couple of words, and then goes and looks one of them up. Then she decides that she needs to know more about some other subject before she can possibly write anything else. By the time she gets round to the writing, there is no time.

3. The writer sits down to work with the subeditor looking over his shoulder. He gets five words into the first sentence and the subeditor tells him he's missed an apostrophe or got words in the wrong order. He deletes the sentence and tries again. This time he gets three words in. Eventually, he's so demoralized that he cannot write a word.

Writer's block is not just a malaise that affects the great prose artists of history but a bug that can reach epidemic proportions at work.

Splurging

The best way to beat writer's block is to allow the writer to work without being interrupted by editors or researchers. This means suspending your critical judgement and just writing whatever comes into your head. I call this 'splurging' – because it's a bit like dumping the contents of your brain on the paper. While I'm splurging, I don't care about the typing mistakes I'm making, I don't care about punctuation, I don't care about my grammar or the structure of my sentences. I don't even care whether I'm making any sense. I allow myself to write in the full knowledge that much of it will be rubbish. The point is that it gets me writing, and it is especially valuable at the beginning of a piece of writing, when I don't yet have anything to go on.

I don't splurge entirely at random, of course; I make sure that I am writing about one of the topics in my plan. But other than that, I leave my brain and my fingers entirely free to put down whatever they want. Once I have some splurged material, I look at it with my editor's hat on. I compare it to the plan I have so far, and I see where it fits. I quite often find that this gives me points that I hadn't thought of before, in the more cerebral activity of editing.

For most people, editing is easier than writing – it is easier to cut and alter and reshape what you have than to get the material down on paper in the first place. That is why you have to redress the balance. Splurging makes writing easy.

Square brackets

Square brackets can be a writer's best friend. They allow you to mark things that are incomplete or unsatisfactory, so that you can return to them later. This means that you can write without feeling that you have to get everything right the first time. I use them in at least four ways:

1. To show that the contents are notes to myself: questions, ideas, comments about the text that follows, etc. They often say things like:

   [perhaps move this paragraph to the beginning of chapter 2].

2. To show that I'm not sure about the sentence inside them. This usually happens if I'm thinking of deleting a sentence but suspect it contains a useful thought that I might want to incorporate in a different form.

3. To show alternatives that I can't decide between. Often these are single words, but they can be whole sentences:

   [I put alternative sentence patterns in square brackets. / Square brackets can be used to show two alternative ways of putting something.]

4. To show that the contents need checking or researching. Rather than breaking my flow to check as

I write, I leave the checking till the end. For example:

When you met Bob [Surname] on [date], you said . . .

All these things have something in common: they are provisional, they call for decisions to be made in a later draft. Other people sometimes use italics or normal brackets for the same purpose, but I think square brackets are better because they are easy to spot. This means that when I've finished writing, I can just do a search (Ctrl and F on a PC, or Apple F on a Mac) for an opening square bracket, and I know it will take me in turn to each problem I need to solve.

Don't delete anything

Another factor that can contribute to writer's block is a reluctance to delete anything or experiment. The best way around this is to keep a copy of more or less every word that you write. If you've been away from the document for a while, or if you're about to make major changes to it, then save a copy, adding to the filename 'd1' (for draft 1) or 'd2', or whatever. Leave that copy untouched and work on the next draft.

An alternative, or accompaniment, to this strategy is to keep what I call a scrapbook.

I always work with two documents open on my computer: one is the document I'm working on, and the other is a scrapbook. Whenever I feel the slightest pang at deleting something, I move it to the scrapbook, so that I know I can easily get it back if I need it. I don't often use anything from this scrapbook, but it comforts me to know that it's there. It means that I can make extensive cuts to my writing without worrying that I'm throwing away good work.

Use paper and pen as well as your computer

If you find you are staring at a blank computer screen, or are finding a particular passage difficult to write, then it can be very therapeutic to write on paper for a bit. Most writers find it helpful to use both pen and keyboard to write. When I don't know where to start, doing a first draft in pen usually gets me going. It is important to have a pen you like. The fluid swish of my fountain pen contributes to the relief of writing on paper, away from the staccato rattle of my keyboard. I don't get the same effect at all from biros, which seem to need dragging across the paper.

Sometimes I start writing with my pen and immediately find that it has given me a spur, and that I now know exactly what I want to say. Then I move back to my keyboard so that I can get it all down quickly. Incidentally, it is well worth learning to touch-type properly: it makes writing on a computer much faster and much more intuitive – it is possible to type almost as quickly as the words come to your mind. When writing with pen, I find my hand often has trouble keeping up with my mind.

Moving between pen and keyboard can also make editing easier. If you are getting confused or disorientated moving blocks of text around on the screen, try printing everything out and editing in ink on the page. You will find that you read more naturally from the page, and you will often spot things on paper that you would have missed on screen. So before you send off anything even remotely important, print it out and check it on paper.

Minimizing computer distractions

Quite a number of professional writers prefer to use older computers, simply because it gives them no option but to write – with no temptation to check emails, browse the Internet, play games or get side-tracked by the thousand other distractions that up-to-date PCs provide. You won't be able to do this at work, but you can minimize one of the main distractions: email.

When I'm writing I keep my email program closed, and only allow myself to start it up and check it at certain times – usually once an hour, or when I take a break. I find that when the email program is running in the background I tend to check it every time a new email arrives, which distracts me from the writing and often breaks my train of thought. There is also, of course, the temptation to respond to the email, which might mean calling someone or looking something up – taking me further away from whatever I was working on originally.

Looking with fresh eyes

One of the main reasons for asking other people to read through your work is that you become blind to what you have written. Joseph Williams, an American writer, says, 'When we read our own stuff, all we're doing is reminding ourselves of what we wanted it to mean when we wrote it.' To minimize this danger, and to read like someone coming to the document for the first time, you need to leave your writing for as long as possible before the final edit. Once you've got a version you're reasonably happy with, leave it in a drawer and don't look at it for a while. If you can, leave it until the next day (or even longer), but even a couple of hours makes a surprising difference to your ability to read it in the same way that other people will.

Summary

- Take on different roles when you write.
- Identify readers, goals and messages before you write.
- Work up a structure and fill it in, or splurge out everything you want to say and then use that to develop a structure.
- Edit for sense and structure before worrying about grammar or punctuation.
- Use square brackets to identify things to sort out later.
- Keep a copy of every draft, and keep a scrapbook of material that you've cut.
- Edit and write with paper and pen as well as on your computer.
- Minimize distractions by closing your email program.
- Try to get someone else to look at your work, or at least talk to someone about it.
- Leave your writing for as long as possible before the final edit.

7

Working in Teams

Writing in teams is becoming a fairly common part of many people's work. It's a very good way of writing a large document very quickly, and it allows you to involve a wide range of different perspectives, talents and specialisms. But it also has its dangers: it can quickly become chaotic and work can be overlooked – especially checking. To minimize these dangers, it is important to have a process that everyone sticks to, and to allocate clear roles and responsibilities.

The process and the roles vary depending on whether you are collaborating on small projects – probably sharing the writing almost equally between two or three people – or working as a team on large projects.

Collaborating on small projects

More or less any document benefits from having more than one person involved, whether it's a letter, a short report or a brochure (see Chapter 5 for a description of the specific requirements of different kinds of documents). In the office, this is often very informal – colleagues casting an eye over each other's work – and it always helps. But things change when you're working together right from the beginning.

The best way to work in a small group is to discuss the job first, talking about the audience, your purpose, your messages and the structure. With these things agreed – and ideally written down, as it can be easy to forget what you said – one of you goes off and writes a first draft, putting their initials at the end of the filename. This first draft might be quite rough, but it gives you something to work with. Save this first try somewhere, because you might need to refer back to it. If you just write over it without saving it separately somewhere, one of you is apt to say at some point, 'I preferred what we had before.' What you had before is likely to be better in your fond imaginings than in reality, but at least if you have the original document you can put it to the test.

Once the first draft has been saved somewhere, send a copy of it to the second person. This person should either give comments and ask for another draft (with a new number) on the basis of them, or have a go himself at editing and amplifying to produce a new draft. If the second person edits it, he should put his initials at the end of the filename, after the first person's initials. This allows you to see how many people's hands the piece has been through. And keeping each draft along the way means that you can always go back and retrieve something if you decide it was working better before.

The essential things are:

- Always explain what you have done and why – it often works best if you sit down together and talk it through. People get demoralized if you change their writing without saying why. Don't just make changes on a whim, but justify them in terms of the overall goal of the piece.
- Decide in advance what kind of tone you want, and which style guide and dictionary you'll use.
- Keep criticism constructive and specific. There's nothing worse than just telling someone that their writing sounds 'poncy' or that it's 'way off the mark' and leaving it at that. Identify specific words, expressions or points and talk about how you think the audience will react to them.

Working on major projects

Some documents can involve almost the whole company: annual reports and proposals for new business (see Chapter 5 for a description) often fall into this category. Although the way of working I describe here would be overkill for some smaller projects, many of the ideas can be applied to pretty much any written work you do. These ideas include version control, clear roles and the distinction between drafting and reviewing.

Clear roles

With projects like these, you need to be disciplined because there is a lot riding on them – sometimes the whole future of the company. In these projects, it becomes even more important to have clear roles and responsibilities, and to stick to a process. On a major project, the main roles are:

- Main writer
- Leader
- Project manager
- Contributors
- Reviewers

Main writer

One of the dangers of having several people contributing to a piece of writing is that the result will be a mish-mash of different styles, approaches and philosophies. The best way around this is to appoint a single person to write and edit. This writer-in-chief's job is to make sure that the result has a consistent feel. She should be prepared to rewrite all contributions, and her word on questions of style should be final – but backed up by a style guide and dictionary. I think it helps a lot if this person is a professional writer, and it helps if she is from outside your company and your industry. An outsider can bring a more objective perspective to the task, and it makes it easier for her to ask 'stupid' questions – to challenge things that might seem self-evident to you, and to question people at the top. Internal people are less likely to want to challenge comfortable assumptions, and they may not want to push for clarification if they fear it could be taken as a sign of ignorance or insolence.

Leader

Another essential is to have someone senior in your organization who is in overall charge of the project – whose word is final when it comes to all the practicalities. It is very important that there be only one person in charge, as this helps to prevent outbreaks of office politics and turf wars, as well as limiting the scope for confusion in the writing. As we'll see in Chapter 8, people have a much harder time writing if they are confused about who their audience is. With just one bigwig to please, things are much easier. The person in overall charge should also have something riding on the end result. If this is a proposal, then the leader of the writing project should be the person who will be responsible for the work (if you win it). If it is a report, then the leader should be the person in whose name the report will be issued.

If the audience is small, the leader should usually be the one who knows them best. Someone this senior is likely to have only a limited amount of time to spend on the project. As a result, the leader may not want to see every draft – perhaps only the first and final drafts. This doesn't matter so long as he sets the overall direction, and gives people a clear idea of what he wants to see.

Project manager

The project manager is in charge of the practical side of things – chasing people up for their contributions or comments, directing research, making sure everyone sticks to the process, ensuring version control (of which more later) and generally keeping people in line.

The project manager also arranges things like printing, binding and distribution – and holds the purse strings.

Contributors

Contributors are responsible for the content (but not the expression or presentation) of a particular subject or section of the document. Whether they submit their material as a first draft, supply rough notes or just make themselves available for interview depends on their preference, their writing ability and the size of the project. Some people like to write something down just to help their thinking, and this material can either be used as a first draft or as the basis for questions in an interview. The essential thing is that contributors know what they're talking about.

Reviewers

Reviewers are the people in the organization to whom the drafts are circulated. They give their opinions on each draft, if required, and any essential disagreements with the overall direction of the project, or with its aims, need to be adjudicated by the leader. You might want to get as much feedback on the first draft as possible, so every contributor may also be a reviewer at this stage. However, the number should shrink with each subsequent draft. Reviewers should know in advance at what stage they will drop out of the reviewing process. Some reviewers will be asked to look at the whole document, while others will just need to look at a particular section, either to make sure it is on the right lines, or to check the technical details at the end.

It helps a lot if, when they are sent the draft, reviewers are given some written guidelines for the kind of comments that are needed. This usually means asking them to ignore typos and points of style – you don't want it to be like getting half a dozen amateur proofreaders to look at an unfinished document. However, they should say if they think the words are misleading or give the wrong impression. You should also ask them to give constructive criticism – not just ripping apart what they read, but giving specific suggestions for improvements.

If you're not getting anything helpful, you might try asking them to give their feedback in a prescribed format, which could include:

• What is best about the document
• Specific ways of improving the document
• An idea that might just be worth trying

Some may want to mark up a copy of the document, giving alternative wording. You should ask them to do this only if they think something is misleading or gives the wrong impression, rather than because they have a chip on their shoulder about *among* and *between* or because they hate split infinitives (see Chapter 14 for explanations).

The process

It may not come as an awful surprise that I believe the process you should follow when writing in a team is pretty much the same as the general process laid out in this book. Begin by looking at yourselves: allocating responsibilities and laying down ground rules, including settling on a single style guide and dictionary. As I suggest in Chapter 12, I recommend *The Economist*'s style-guide and *The Penguin Dictionary*.

Next, think about your audience. Go through Chapter 2 to identify the people you need to concentrate on and to write down everything you know about them, what they will want to read and why. Then decide what you want your audience to do as a result of reading your document, how you want it to affect them. Use chapters 3 and 4 to move from this to your general messages and a basic structure for your document. Then allocate different parts of this structure to different contributors and set a deadline for the first draft. This first draft doesn't have to be great, and some of it may be in note form, but it should give the reviewers a reasonable feel for the content, the structure, the strategy and the tone you intend for the finished document. This means that it's important to include:

- A draft executive summary that you're reasonably happy with. This is the most important element of the first draft. It enables reviewers to judge the tone, and to decide whether they think it needs to be warmer, lighter or more formal. It also allows reviewers to see all the main messages in one place, giving them a good way of judging the content of the whole document.
- A table of contents, so that reviewers can judge the structure and decide whether they're happy with the section headings and the order in which things are brought up.
- A plan of each section containing descriptions or

mock-ups of any charts, data or graphics that you plan to include, along with a list of subheadings and key points.

- A note on the planned design and presentation, with a mock-up if possible, so that reviewers can decide whether it fits the text, the audience and the image your organization wants to project. An increasing number of companies have very strict brand guidelines which lay down what colours, fonts and layouts must be used.

- A briefing note on the audience and your aims, so that reviewers can see why you've approached the project as you have, and can contribute any extra knowledge they have about the audience.

It can be useful if the main writer makes messages more extreme in the drafts than they would be in the final edit. It helps you to find out for sure about people's sensitivities and bugbears, and it means that the inevitable watering down that occurs during review may not entirely erase all humanity from the document.

Keeping track of drafts

Keeping track of the different drafts in a collaborative project is essential, and is often referred to by the rather grand phrase *version control*. After the document has been sent to the reviewers, all work on that draft stops. If it is the first draft, add 'd1' (signifying draft 1) to the filename and save it in a folder called drafts – you may need to refer back to it later, when someone says they preferred what they had before. Save another copy of the file with the suffix 'd2' and work on that until the next time it's sent out for review, when you will file it again and begin work on d3.

The reason for this strictness is to avoid having different people working on different versions. There's nothing worse than someone coming to you with a set of detailed comments and amendments they've made to a document printed out three drafts ago that no longer bears any relation to the one you're working on now. Trying to reconcile changes to different drafts is much more difficult than reconciling different people's work on the same draft. The project manager and the main writer should both be completely humourless and autocratic when it comes to version control.

Another thing that's very important for maintaining version control is to have only one person who is allowed to make changes to the 'live' document. Everyone else contributes comments, revisions, additions and suggestions, but no one should change the document itself. If people want to edit the document, they should make it very clear what they want to change, how and why. If you are using Microsoft Word, as most people do at work, then the 'Track changes' feature can be very useful.

You will need to set a strict deadline for the reviewers to submit their comments. Don't fall into the trap of beginning to revise a section of the document before you have all the comments back for that section – the last reviewer might completely change your ideas about what needs to be done. There are, in any case, usually plenty of other things to be getting on with. For the writer, taking a rest can be the best use of time while you're waiting for feedback. As the deadline approaches, the work gets more frantic, and last-minute revisions and responding to new information often mean staying up all night at the end.

Reconciling everyone else's feedback can be a big job, especially on the first draft, which goes out in the least complete state to the largest number of reviewers. If reviewers' feedback is incompatible, the project manager should get them to discuss it with one another, and if they can't agree – or if their agreement flies in the face of the overall plan – he should refer the question to the leader to decide. Once all the feedback is in, it is the writer's job to make the necessary changes.

How it works
To sum up, this is how I recommend running a large writing project:

Phase	Actions
1. Kick off	• Appoint a writer, project manager and leader.
2. Strategy	• Identify the audience.
	• Decide what you want them to do.
	• Formulate key messages to achieve that.
	• Take account of any specific requirements – such as a brief from your client or a Request for Proposals document.
	• Plan the structure.
	• Allocate tasks to contributors.
	• Summarize your knowledge of your audience and your approach.
	• Write a design brief for the way you want your document to look.

Phase	Actions
	• Appoint reviewers and say clearly when they will drop out of the process. • The project manager should work out a timetable (remember that the first draft usually takes longest).
3. Drafting	• The writer drafts material supplied by the contributors. • The project manager organizes and chases up contributors. • At a predetermined deadline, work on the draft ceases and it is sent out to the reviewers. • The old draft is saved, and a new draft is begun to take account of the reviewers' comments.
4. Reviewing	• The reviewers look at the latest draft and make comments – on a hard copy in pen, on a soft copy using MS Word's 'track changes' tool, on a feedback form or in a short piece of writing. • There is a deadline for them to submit their comments. • Sometimes, especially at the beginning and right at the end, it can be useful for the reviewers to have a meeting with the writer, project manager and leader. If so, someone needs to take notes, and the actions or changes that arise need to be written down and agreed upon.

Drafting and reviewing alternate until the document is finished.
This might mean four or five drafts – or even more.

5. Semi-final draft	• The text is pasted into the document design.
	• All graphics are included.
6. Final draft	• The writer, project manager and leader go through the document together, page by page. They may ask some specialist reviewers to be there too.
	• Once everyone is happy with the words, the writer or a specialist proofreader checks the whole document.
	• The document is printed and distributed.

This is, admittedly, an idealized description of the process. In reality, it doesn't always work like this. It isn't always possible to get someone – the right someone – to work as project manager, and it then becomes harder and harder to chase people up and to maintain strict version control. However, the more nearly a big team project approximates to this process, the better it will be.

For me, the project that came closest to the ideal was when I was the writer on a media group's proposal to one of the big power companies. Things went pretty much exactly as I've described above, with the result that an independent auditor of all the proposals said that ours was the best they'd ever read. But, as is the way of these things, we still didn't win the contract. Although a poor proposal can lose you a contract, a good proposal alone is not enough to win one. It has to be backed up by a good relationship with your prospective client, by the right fee structure and – especially for larger deals – by good politics.

Summary

- Always save different drafts separately:
  - Give them different draft numbers
  - Add the initials of the last person to work on it
- Agree the basics before you start:
  - Who your audience is
  - What your goal is
  - What your messages are
  - What tone you want
  - Which style guide and dictionary you'll use
  - Who is going to check the document at the end
- Keep criticism of other people's work constructive and specific.
- On larger projects, agree clear roles:
  - Main writer
  - Leader
  - Project manager
  - Contributors
  - Reviewers

Part 2

Your Writing: Making It Clear and Easy to Read

There's something about writing at work that seems to encourage people to make their sentences lumpy and difficult to follow. Perhaps it's the sense that writing at work is functional, and therefore needn't concern itself with good writing. Perhaps people see elegance as a frippery best left to poets and 'creative writers'.

They shouldn't see it that way: all writing is creative. Writing at work doesn't need to be beautiful, but it must – above all – be clear. After all, what utility is there in writing that doesn't get its message across? Take a look at the example below:

Set against the background of these profound changes have been emerging trends of reduced state participation in the Norwegian oilfields and a recognition of the need to encourage competition in a sector that has been strongly impacted by recent merger activity.

You might work out what it is saying, but it takes an effort to do so. If you force your reader to make this effort in sentence after sentence, they will – sooner rather than later – give up the unequal struggle. You will then have lost the chance to communicate with them and to influence them. Now read the version below:

While these changes have been happening, the state has begun to reduce its involvement in the Norwegian oilfields. It now recognizes that, because so many companies have merged, it must encourage competition.

If you find the second version easier to understand, it is because it focuses on telling you *who* did *what*. In the second version, it is quite clear *who* we are talking about – it is the state. In the first version, there are several candidates: is it the background? The profound changes? The emerging trends? State participation? It's difficult to say. And what is the state doing? In the second version it is reducing its involvement in the Norwegian oilfields. In the first version, it is, again, difficult to say.

These are the two essential pieces of information a reader needs in any sentence:

- Who: the subject of the sentence. This tells us what the writer is talking about here – whether it's a person (John Miles, our CEO), an organization (the Norwegian state, Microsoft) or a concept (efficiency, risk-based auditing).
- What: the action of the sentence. This tells us what happened – what did the subject do? John Miles *gave*

a speech. The Norwegian state *reduced its involvement in the oilfield*. Risk-based auditing *saved us money*.

The more you can make these things leap out at the reader, the more comprehensible people will find your writing, the more they will read it, the better they will understand it, and the more effective it will be. The more effective your writing is, the more valuable you will become, and the higher your rewards will be. This might sound obvious, but a surprising number of people ignore it.

In this section, I will look at these two essential parts of any sentence, before going on to discuss the tone you take – or how your words will sound to your reader – and the length of your sentences.

8
Who: Making Your Subject Clear

Following a six-year study of high-growth companies and their less successful competitors, Kim and Mauborgne suggested that high-growth companies paid little attention to beating their rivals, but instead sought to make their competitors irrelevant by fundamentally rethinking the sources of value (especially customer value) in their industry and then reconfiguring products offer, services offer, delivery platforms, assets, and capabilities to deliver that value at significant levels of profit.

One of the many problems with this epic sentence is that it skips about from subject to subject – it can never quite decide whether it is talking about the study, Kim and Mauborgne, the high-growth companies, their industry or its sources of value. One of the most effective ways of making your sentences clearer is to deal with just one subject in each, and to be absolutely clear about what that subject is.

Here's what happens when we do that to the sentence above:

Kim and Mauborgne spent six years studying companies to see what made them grow. They found that the companies with highest growth focused not on beating their competitors, but on making them irrelevant. These high-growth companies looked afresh at what people in their industry (especially customers) were willing to pay for. They then changed their products and services – and the way they provided them – accordingly, even if it meant buying or selling assets and learning to do new things.

The 69-word sentence above has become a four-sentence paragraph, growing by a modest 10 words in the process. Overall, writing clearly and directly will mean that you use fewer words, but this isn't always true for individual sentences. We have now rationalized the number of subjects to just two: high-growth companies, and Kim and Mauborgne.

A good way to reduce and clarify the number of subjects in your writing is to ask: *Who is taking action here?* Asking that question of the original sentence, we find that the six-year study doesn't really *do* anything, and neither do the industry or the sources of value. It's no coincidence that all these things are abstract, inanimate objects that are difficult to imagine. Far better to talk about people, such as Kim and Mauborgne, and human organizations made up of people, such as the high-growth companies. Readers understand best when they can picture something, when they can see it in their mind's eye. That's why it's always best to talk about people and solid things whenever you can.

Having identified your subject, you should put it right at the beginning of the sentence. It's fine to use a scene-setter – such as *however* or *while these changes have been happening* – but the sooner we find a clear subject, the better.

Introducing and explaining

These subjects are a bit like the cast of characters in a play. You need to keep them to a minimum, or the audience will forget who they are and get them mixed up. And, just as every character in a play needs to be introduced, so do the subjects in your writing.

If, in the example above, it were the first time we had heard the names Kim and Mauborgne, we would need to say who they are:

Kim and Mauborgne, two leading US economists, spent six years . . .

Or, if there's no particular need for your readers to remember the names, but you want to give them just for reference, you might give the description first:

Two leading US economists, Kim and Mauborgne, spent six years . . .

In this second example, you would probably refer to 'the economists' thereafter, because that's how you've introduced them. In the first example, you would use their names. You will also sometimes see – especially in newspapers – a description being given as though it were the person's title: *Prime minister Tony Blair* or *Leading US economists Kim and Mauborgne*. It is best not to do this, because it can be confusing to read. However, you can use any of these techniques to establish early on a short and simple way of referring to your subject, so that rather than repeating *Kim and Mauborgne*, you can say *the two economists*. Once you've established this, stick to it.

Names – and company-specific terms

It is always worth going back and checking through your writing to make sure that you have introduced everyone and explained what everything is.

Ben and Saranjit reported on our work for DoH on choice and disadvantage at a workshop in February. Our research findings will be published as part of our 2004/5 workplan.

It is easy to forget that not everyone knows Ben and Saranjit as well as you do, and so we need surnames and titles or descriptions in order to understand what is going on:

Ben Burnside, our CEO, and Saranjit Kapla, our head of marketing, reported on our work for the Department of Health (DoH) . . .

But there's something else wrong with this extract: the uninitiated reader won't see the connection between the two sentences. 'What research findings?' the reader will ask. 'And what is a workplan?'

The writer here knows that the company's work for the Department of Health was a research project, and so naturally makes the leap, but the reader has to infer it. Also, the writer hasn't realized that what is an everyday term to him – *workplan* – might not be familiar to his readers. Readers might imagine from the context that it is a published annual plan of the company's work.

In fact, this company uses the word much more loosely to refer to all the things they do in a given year. To avoid these problems the writer could have written:

Ben Burnside, our CEO, and Saranjit Kapla, our head of marketing, reported on our work for the Department of Health (DoH) at a workshop in February. This work consisted of research into choice and disadvantage, and it will be published in full later this year.

All companies and organizations have their equivalents of *workplan* – terms that are used every day by everyone in the company, terms that sound self-explanatory, but aren't. Terms like these are often the biggest barriers between you and your readers, which means that you need to keep a constant eye out for them. If you have really thought hard about who your readers are, it will be much easier for you to identify the words and phrases that are likely to mystify them. But even so, these words will often be so deeply ingrained that the only reliable way of rooting them out is to read through your document asking yourself, at every step of the way, 'Does this word mean the same thing to my readers as it does to me?'

The things you should be looking out for are:

- People – have you introduced them, with titles and surnames, and explained why they are relevant to the reader?
- Offices – how are they relevant to the reader? One thing to look out for here is the common practice of using the name or location of an office to refer to its function: writing *Broadgate* when you mean *our*

headquarters, or *Chichester* when you mean *our finance department*.

- Departments – be wary of assuming that your readers know all about your internal organization. If your readers work in another company, they may very well look at markets or industry sectors, for example, in a different way than you do. In your company, renewable energy might be dealt with by the Oil and Gas Practice, which could mystify readers unless you explain it.
- Products – companies often have a vast array of products which they are keen to mention at every opportunity. However, it is not always a good idea. If you are writing about one or two products, or for an internal audience, then by all means use your trademarked product names. But if you overwhelm your readers with mystifying names such as KV143OUB (a TV) or ZoomDirector (a way of planning which advertising space to buy), they will remember none of them.

It is always worth considering whether you need to use a name at all. For a single, brief mention, it can be easier for the reader if you use the description on its own. If, in the example above, Ben and Saranjit were not mentioned again, then it would be easier to leave out their names altogether:

Our CEO and our head of marketing reported on our work for the Department of Health (DoH) at a workshop in February.

We might not even need this much detail. Perhaps it doesn't matter who did the reporting:

We reported on our work for the Department of Health (DoH) at a workshop in February.

You can do your readers a service by not giving them any more information than they need.

Abbreviations and acronyms

Abbreviations and acronyms are a fact of modern life, a useful shorthand way of referring to complex ideas. However, they are often used carelessly, without explanation, and in such profusion that they get in the way of readers' understanding, rather than helping them. The purpose of brevity is not to save you typing, but to present information to your readers in the most direct and efficient way.

Incidentally, an abbreviation is only an acronym, strictly speaking, when it can be said as a word. So radar, EBITDA and RAM are acronyms, but GDP and PC aren't. There is no generally recognized word for expressions made from the first letters of the words in a phrase, although some people call them 'initialisms'.

The following example comes from an article that is attempting to persuade companies to choose a particular technology for storing information on computer networks:

SANs are much more cost-effective than DAS environments, providing an extremely fast ROI. Many SAN implementations pay for themselves in six months or less.

The standard approach is to give definitions in brackets when an abbreviation is first used, even if you are fairly sure your audience will know what it stands for:

SANs (storage area networks) are much more cost-effective than DAS (direct attached storage) environments, providing an extremely fast ROI (return on investment). Many SAN implementations pay for themselves in six months or less.

If the first mention is plural, make the definition plural:

SANs (storage area networks) are . . .

If the first mention is a possessive, make the definition possessive:

Our SAN's (storage area network's) greatest benefit is . . .

But try hard to rewrite the sentence to avoid having to do this.

Giving definitions in brackets works well when there are relatively few abbreviations (two or three per page is the maximum), and when readers are relatively familiar with them. When the unfamiliar abbreviations begin to multiply, a different approach is required. The following paragraph is taken from a report on the European Rail Traffic Management System by the Strategic Rail Authority (soon to be abolished). It is describing one of the three main reasons for using the system, and is intended for public consumption:

Safety – a means of providing ATP to further reduce the incidence and consequences of SPADs, which as explained, is why Uff/Cullen recommended the adoption of ERTMS. As TPWS significantly mitigates ATP-preventable risks, the relatively small additional risk reduction achieved by ERTMS (once TPWS is installed) appears not to be justified purely as a safety investment. However, providing a signal in the train cab through the use of ERTMS will be a major step forward for drivers, particularly at high speeds in complex layouts, and under adverse weather conditions. ERTMS will also facilitate improved possession management and require less trackside infrastructure, thus reducing risks to trackside workers.

All these terms are defined somewhere in the report, but readers cannot possibly be expected to remember so many definitions in such a short time. Readers have to make an active effort to recall terms such as SPAD, ATP, TPWS and Uff/Cullen – or go back and find the page where they were defined. However, simply repeating the definitions doesn't help much:

Safety – a means of providing ATP (Automatic Train Protection) to further reduce the incidence and consequences of SPADs (signals passed at danger), which as explained, is why Uff/Cullen (the report from the joint inquiry into train protection systems, chaired by Professor Uff and Lord Cullen, following the accidents at Southall in 1997 and Ladbroke Grove in 1999) recommended the adoption of ERTMS (European Rail Traffic Management System). As TPWS (Train Protection and Warning System) significantly mitigates . . .

The writers of this document could have made it much more friendly and useful (and therefore effective) by just thinking about what they were saying, and giving explanations rather than abbreviations:

Safety

Uff and Cullen's inquiry recommended adopting ERTMS because it will mean fewer danger signals going unheeded. But, by itself, this reduction would not justify the cost, because ERTMS is only slightly more effective than the Train

Protection and Warning System in this respect. The advantage of ERTMS is that its signals go directly to the drivers' cabs, which is particularly helpful when trackside signals are difficult to see: at high speeds, in complex track layouts and in bad weather. Eliminating these trackside signals would save money and administration – as well as reducing the risks to the workers who maintain them.

By getting rid of abbreviations and technical terms, we've made the text much more readable and comprehensible. We've done this partly by being clear about the subject of each sentence, and partly by reducing the number of different terms. Now, the only abbreviation is ERTMS, which is fitting, since it is the subject of the report. Other concepts are referred to in everyday terms: they are described rather than named. This reduces the number of characters our readers have to remember. Because we are making fewer demands on them, they will find the text easier, quicker and more rewarding to read.

The first change is to the way the paragraph is set up. In the original, the word *safety* is followed by a dash, which makes it look as though what follows will be a brief definition. Instead what follows is a detailed discussion, so *safety* works better as a heading.

In the first sentence, the main change is to identify a useful subject. There are several candidates, but I chose *Uff/Cullen*. By spelling this out as *Uff and Cullen's inquiry*, I have brought people into the text. I got rid of the term *SPADs* because they are not things that can be visualized. Even spelled out – *signals passed at danger* – the reader has to make an effort. The answer is to turn this abstract term into a concrete situation: danger signals going unheeded.

The second sentence of the original is disorientating because it suddenly introduces a new subject – TPWS – without saying how it relates to what we have already been told. It has a vague action, *significantly mitigates*, followed by another mystifying term: *ATP-preventable risk*. A close reading tells us that the risks ATP prevents are signals passed at danger, the reduction of which was mentioned at the end of the first sentence. This allows us to begin this sentence by talking about *this reduction*. We start the sentence *But* to show that it contrasts with the first one: in the first sentence ERTMS was recommended, in the second we learn that the cost is not justified.

The third sentence (beginning *However*) also introduces something unfamiliar and again fails to tell us explicitly how it relates to what we already know. What we already know is that an inquiry recommended using ERTMS, but that the cost of ERTMS can't be justified only by its reduction of the number of danger signals that drivers pass. Now we are being told how the cost of ERTMS might be justified – the signal in the train cab – so the beginning of the sentence must communicate this.

A major step forward for drivers is not an evocative phrase, and it does not explicitly say what the benefits for drivers are, or why they would be particularly noticeable *at high speeds in complex layouts and under adverse weather conditions*. The point is that ERTMS sends signals straight to the train cab (I call it the *driver's cab* to save words), so the driver doesn't have to rely on signals by the side of the track, which can be difficult to see. I then use a colon to introduce a list of the circumstances in which trackside signals can be difficult to see. And I have added the word *track* to *complex layouts* because it isn't immediately obvious to the layman that this is the kind of layout the writer had in mind. There are also some typically verbose phrases in this sentence that can be written more simply: *Under adverse weather conditions* means nothing more than 'in bad weather'.

In the final sentence, the other benefits of ERTMS are all consequences of the elimination of trackside signals, but the original does not draw out this connection. By making the connection clear, the point becomes much easier to grasp. Making a piece of writing flow depends on demonstrating and explaining the connections, consequences and contrasts between the different things you mention. In addition, describing things and spelling them out – *danger signals going unheeded, the Train Protection and Warning System, Uff and Cullen's inquiry* – rather than using abbreviations, makes the text self-explanatory. And because it also loosens the text up, the second version is shorter than the first.

Making your writing less complex and technical

I shortened the extract above mainly by replacing unfamiliar or technical terms with simple explanations. The result communicates the meaning far better without seeming simplistic. Making writing less complex and technical is a very effective way of making it more readable and easier to understand. Unfortunately, many people exert their efforts in the opposite direction: because they spend their working lives trying to project an image of themselves as knowledgeable and technically proficient insiders, they try to make everything as complex, abstract and technical as possible.

The results are often laughable – at least until you consider the massive cost: the inefficiency, the time, the money, the avoidable mistakes and the confusion. The extract below comes from a glossary of business terms provided by Gemini Consulting. It's likely that their clients did need such a glossary, but unfortunately they would have needed another glossary to understand the definitions. This won the Business Jargon Competition run by the *Financial Times* newspaper and the Management Consultancies' Association:

Referential Transparency

The result of contextualisation. Prospectively, a system wherein all parts are connected by a self-similar ruleset; retrospectively, that system wherein the prospective connections are observed as syntax.

It's almost impossible to tell, but I think it means something like this:

Clear references put things in context. They follow a consistent system of rules that not only are clear in hindsight, but can be seen in advance.

Gemini's client must have paid at least twice for this nonsense: once for the expensive consultant who wrote it and again for the time the client's employees wasted reading it and trying to decipher what it means.

If you're not sure what it means, don't write it

A small number of companies dominate the market, which means high market concentration and limited competition.

The person who wrote this obviously didn't know what the term *high market concentration* means, because it means nothing more nor less than that a small number of companies dominate the market; if you've said the latter, there's no need to say the former. The writer obviously just used the phrase because she thought it sounded impressive. But using words and phrases you don't understand is pointless: the people you most need to impress are precisely the people who are least likely to be taken in by it.

One of the most common reasons for writing poorly is that the writer literally doesn't know what he means by his words. The writing is difficult to understand because it doesn't mean anything. By getting you to identify what you want to say, why and to whom, the first part of this book should solve this problem, but it is essential that you become aware of the words you are using. Do you really know what they mean? Why have you used that particular word and not another?

Ask yourself these questions as you read through your work. When coaching people on their writing, I find that when I ask people, 'What does that mean?' they almost always give a clear and simple explanation more or less straight away. 'So why not write that?' is always my next question. It is a very good discipline: if you use words and expressions in writing that you wouldn't use in conversation, then it is always a sign that something is wrong. If you write as you speak, you're doing something right.

Confusing subjects

We have looked at some ways of making the subject of your sentence clear, so now let's look at some of the most common ways of obscuring it: lists, abstract terms and passive sentences.

Lists

Protracted uncertainty over petrol prices, recent financial scandals, continued threat of global terrorism, structural problems in European economies, all are badly affecting confidence of business, investors, consumers alike.

There are two main problems with this sentence: it begins with a list and it ends with another list. The problem with beginning a sentence with a list is that it makes it difficult for the reader to find her feet in the sentence, to orientate herself. A good sentence tells you straight away exactly what it is going to talk about, but a list gives you too many candidates. What's worse, this list is ambiguous. Does *protracted uncertainty over* relate just to petrol prices, or to recent financial scandals and the threat of global terrorism? Does *continued threat of* apply just to global terrorism or to the structural problems too? A bit of thought tells you that both these expressions relate only to the term that immediately follows, but we don't want our readers to have to think about things like this. We want them to be thinking about our messages, not trying to work out what those messages are. To avoid this, order your list so that the most complex items go last – especially if, like the ones above, they have words like *over*, *of* or *in* in them. This is the least confusing form of the list above:

. . . recent financial scandals, structural problems in European economies, the continued threat of global terrorism, and protracted uncertainty over petrol prices . . .

If you insist on beginning a sentence with a list, make sure there are no more than three items in it, that each item is a single word, and that they are all part of a recognizable category. The example above would be much better if it were flipped around:

Businesses, investors and consumers have all had their confidence shaken by recent financial scandals, structural problems in European economies, the continued threat of global terrorism, and protracted uncertainty over petrol prices.

The first thing people read affects their comprehension of everything that follows. In general, it is best to start with something short and simple that more or less sums up your message. Then, once people have the overall structure, you can fill in the details. Our original example follows the opposite pattern: it gives readers a list of detailed information and then it tells them what to do with it. This means that readers have to hold all that information in their heads while they await further instructions: an uncomfortable position to be in, and one which makes considerable demands on short-term memory. Forcing your readers to use their short-term memories in this way will tire them. It will be even more difficult for them if their concentration is impaired by other factors, such as fatigue, stress and distractions. At work, you can pretty much guarantee that your readers will be coping with all these things.

Here's what happens when we rewrite our example with this in mind:

Confidence has fallen among businesses, investors and consumers. The causes include recent financial scandals, structural problems in European economies, the continued threat of global terrorism, and protracted uncertainty over petrol prices.

It is still not a thing of beauty, but it is unquestionably easier to understand than the original.

Abstraction

Abstraction is a natural consequence of the urge to sound important. It is also caused by a lack of confidence. See how self-important and defensive this writer sounds as she explains to a customer why her company won't be upgrading its computers:

This issue has been turned aside as the benefit of the upgrade would affect so few of our customer base. As such there are no plans, at present, for this improvement to be made.

Why are we talking about a *customer base*, rather than *customers*? I know what customers are: they are people like you and me. I can imagine customers, I can picture them in my mind's eye. I cannot picture a customer base except perhaps as some vague diagram from a long-forgotten business-studies textbook. Here's how www.small-business-dictionary.org defines the term:

For a business, its total list of customers, total number of potential customers or group of customers with specific classification characteristics. Such customer-base identification allows more accurate targeting of marketing objectives.

In this case, as in many others, using the abstract term is not only more confusing, but also less accurate. And, whatever else a customer base is, it is singular, so the word 'few' is wrong.

There are several other problems with this example. The writer has used *as such* wrongly. *As such* means, more or less, 'in itself' or 'because it is what it is'. So, *I don't object to privatization as such* means 'I don't object to privatization simply because it is privatization.' Or, in the example *She is our marketing manager, and as such she should decide where we advertise*, *as such* means 'as she is our marketing manager'. However, more and more people use it just as a filler in their writing, a sort of upmarket 'like, y'know'.

This example would seem much more honest and confident if it used concrete expressions, rather than abstractions, and if it just laid things on the line:

We have decided not to upgrade our computers because so few customers would benefit from it.

We have clearly identified who is doing something (*we*) and what they are doing (*deciding*), and then we give the reason. With an apology for the inconvenience, the customer could not ask for anything more.

In the example above, adding the word *base* to the otherwise straightforward *customers* is what takes it from the concrete world that we live in and can visualize, to the abstract plane where nothing is what it seems. There are plenty of ways of doing this, and all of them are easy to remedy. A client of mine used always to tell customers who complained:

I have now had the opportunity to investigate the background to your complaint.

Note that he hasn't investigated, he's merely had the opportunity, and it isn't the complaint itself he has tackled, but merely the background to it. It sounds much more positive and active to say:

I have investigated your complaint.

Another client always used the phrase *levels of*, which made his writing more abstract. *Increasing someone's involvement* – or just *getting someone more involved* would be transmuted into *enhancing* their *levels of involvement*. Here's another example:

Following significant investment in facilities enhanced levels of customer convenience will be delivered.

This makes convenience sound like a substance that can be measured out by the millilitre and left on your doorstep with the milk rather than something that makes people's lives easier. As before, the remedy is simply to get rid of the words *levels of* that make the phrase abstract. Again, it also helps to have a clear subject:

We will invest a significant amount of money to make our facilities more convenient for customers.

This example is from a press release from the Office of Fair Trading:

The OFT today announced that it is to consult with the home credit industry on making a market investigation reference to the Competition Commission (CC).

Making a market investigation reference to the Competition Commission is the same thing as *referring a market to the CC for investigation*, or just *asking the Competition Commission to investigate a market*.

The OFT announced today that it is to consult the home credit industry about the possibility of asking the Competition Commission to investigate it.

It is usually worth considering the order in which you bring things up. In this case, the sense that this is the home credit industry's last chance to avert an investigation might be communicated better this way:

The OFT announced today that it is considering asking the Competition Commission to investigate the home credit market, but that it will first consult companies in the industry.

Passives

You may have noticed that in rewriting some of the examples above I introduced a *we* where there had not previously been one. I did that because writing is most comprehensible when it talks about people taking actions. Without the people, things 'just happen'. In the first example above, we learned that *this issue has been turned aside*, but no one told us *who* turned it aside.

This is a passive sentence:

Research was carried out by government scientists.

Research here is in the position where we would usually expect to find the subject of the sentence, the element of it that took action. But in this sentence, *research* doesn't take any action; instead, scientists act upon it.

We can find out who the subject of the sentence is by asking 'Who performed the action?' In this case, it was the government scientists. Then we ask 'What did they do?' They carried out research. So we can turn it into an active sentence:

Government scientists carried out research.

People take less time to read active sentences than passive ones, which are almost always more difficult to understand. If the elements of the passive sentence are long and complex, then the extra effort the reader has to make becomes significant.

The main problem with passive sentences is that it is possible to leave out the subject altogether and just say:

Research was carried out.

This passive sentence is grammatically correct, but it leaves out a piece of crucial information: who acted.

There can be good reasons for leaving this information out. The main reason is to avoid shifting the focus of the sentence unnecessarily. For example, if we were writing about Jaguar, the car company, it would probably be better to say:

Jaguar was acquired by Ford in 1989.

than to say:

Ford acquired Jaguar in 1989.

The second of those sentences makes it sound as though the whole piece of writing is going to be about Ford rather than Jaguar.

So long as you know why you are doing it, there is nothing wrong with using a passive sentence. But in business (or in any institution) it is easy to slip into the habit of using the passive all the time. I think that this is because passives are often used in scientific and academic writing to make the writer seem objective. Passives remove people, and scientists are very keen to show that they simply observed and didn't affect the results. They naturally want to erase themselves from the picture. Of course, this is a fallacy, since it *is* scientists who carry out the experiments they record, and it is very easy for them to unwittingly affect the results. So even in this sphere, it would be better to lose the habitual passive.

People in many other walks of life want to take on the mantle of science, to benefit from its air of authority and objectivity. This is one reason why people get into the habit of writing in the passive. It is also partly out of defensiveness: because they do not want to accept liability or be seen to cast blame. This is usually counterproductive: writing becomes a series of things 'just happening' with no one taking any actions. This makes writing unreadable and very difficult to follow. It also gives the impression that the writer is faceless, inhuman, evasive and does not know what is going on. This is not usually a good idea. If a customer complains to a company because its actions (or lack of them) have upset him, he is likely to become more angry and upset if the reply implies that no one has taken any decisions or actions. Using passives makes this implication.

Only use a passive for a good reason. Don't get into the habit of writing passively, but think hard about each one. A passive is acceptable if:

- You want to keep the focus of the sentence on the person or thing to whom something is happening, rather than the one who is taking the action: *Jaguar was acquired by Ford*.
- You want to imply that something has 'just happened' without anyone intending it to: *It was blown down*.
- You deliberately want to avoid saying who did something, either because you don't know or because it would be rude to do so: *Her wallet was stolen*.

Perhaps the oddest thing about the pervasiveness of passives is that they are so easy to turn into good active sentences. Because they're so easy to change, I've provided three examples:

1. *It was agreed that you would pay this back in four instalments of £50.*
   Here, the crucial point is that the customer had agreed to do this. If the company had agreed this unilaterally, no one could have blamed the customer for not repaying the money. The solution:

You agreed to pay this back in four instalments of £50.

2. *It is regretted that you have had problems.*

If you want to sound insincere, use a passive sentence. Nothing beats their combination of feebleness, anonymity and inaction. Who regrets that the customer has had problems? We don't know. Here, combining the passive with a thin, weedy verb like 'to regret' puts the icing on the cake. The solution:

I am sorry that you have had problems.

3. *The original order cannot be located.*

Again, this is from a response to a customer's complaint. It is a fairly central point whether the customer or the company lost the order, so it is vital to be clear which it is. This passive makes it sound as though it is the order's fault that it cannot be located. The solution:

We cannot find the original order.

The moral is that if you can say who did what, then do. In every case, you just need to ask:

Who did this?   That is the subject.
What did they do?   That is the verb.
To whom did they do it?   That is the object.

The guideline is:

A sentence is clear if it says who did what.

Sentences that don't focus on one thing

Finally, it's worth going through and checking each *they* and *it* in your writing. Again, your readers will usually be able to work out what you meant, but you can save them the effort:

The directors recommend that shareholders vote in favour of these new resolutions as they intend to do.

A moment's thought will tell the reader that *they* refers to the directors, rather than the shareholders – after all, why would the directors recommend something that will happen anyway? But that moment's thought adds to the impression of difficulty in your writing. If you sort out any ambiguities in your writing, then the effort has to be made only once. Often you can rewrite the sentence so that *they* or *it* can only refer to one thing:

The directors intend to vote in favour of the motion, and they recommend that shareholders do the same.

The ambiguity is usually more irritating than genuinely confusing, but the result can be unintentionally hilarious, as in this famous example:

When Her Majesty had broken the traditional bottle of champagne over the bows of the ship, she slid slowly and gracefully down the slipway, entering the water with scarcely a splash.

Summary

- Each sentence should have a single, clear subject – the person or thing taking action.
- Reduce and clarify the number of subjects in your writing by asking 'Who is taking action here?' Try to put that at the beginning of the sentence.
- Take people as your subjects wherever possible. Failing that, make your subjects things that your readers can imagine and identify with, such as groups, organizations, or everyday things that can be seen and touched.

- Always introduce and explain things when you first mention them. Look out for people, offices, departments and products.
- Read through your writing and ask, every step of the way, 'Does this word mean the same thing to my readers as it does to me?'
- Don't introduce something new without explaining how it relates to what went before.

- When you first use an acronym or abbreviation, spell it out in brackets after the word.
- If you have more than two or three acronyms and abbreviations on a page, then try to replace them with everyday descriptions.

- Try not to begin a sentence with a list.
- Try not to have more than three or four items in a list.
- Keep each list item simple. Put longer or more complex items at the end of the list.

- Be direct. Don't write words or expressions that you wouldn't use in conversation.
- Never use a word just to make yourself feel important.
- Write about what people will actually see and experience. Instead of *delivering enhanced levels of convenience* to your readers, make their lives easier.

- Avoid passive sentences, such as *Research was carried out*. Instead, say who did what: *Scientists carried out research*.
- Only use a passive for a very good reason:
  - To keep the focus of the sentence on the person or thing to whom the action is happening
  - To imply that something has 'just happened' without anyone intending it to
  - To avoid saying who did something, either because you don't know or because it would be rude to say

9
What: Clear Actions

We have completed the undertaking in a timely manner of high-level and detailed discussions of the current situation.

In this example it is clear what the subject is: whatever is being done, *we* are doing it. But try to find out what the action is, try to pinpoint exactly what is happening, and you find it is much less certain. Is *have* the action? No, the sentence is not about something that *we* own, so look to the next word. Is *completed* the action? Does that get to the heart of what is happening in this sentence? No, the burden of the sentence is not conveyed by the word *completed*. Is it *undertaking*? No, again that doesn't tell you very much. Is the action conveyed by the phrase *we have completed the undertaking*? No, that also tells you very little. In fact, we don't get to the key action word until almost the end of the sentence. *Discussion* is the main action here.

We can make this sentence much clearer by putting the main action immediately after the subject. Who is taking action here? *We* are. What are *we* doing? *Discussing*.

We discussed the current situation in detail.

This gives you all the information you need (although it would be even better to say what the current situation is). The rest is padding.

Padding

Sometimes almost the whole sentence is padding, and you never reach a concrete and specific action:

Guernsey prides itself on being able to deliver core levels of effectiveness, and continuous evaluation of the Island's ability to deliver in a competitive context is encouraged by the local Government and commercial enterprise alike.

Again, in this example it is clear what the subject is: it is Guernsey. But what Guernsey is doing is almost impossible to say. The sentence sounds plausible enough and there is nothing wrong with it grammatically, but ask yourself what is happening and you will find that you are none the wiser. What is the action here? Is it *to pride oneself*? Not really: that's a prelude, a way of introducing the action. Cut through the padding and the main verb seems to be *to deliver*. But *deliver* is being used in a vague, abstract way. Guernsey is not delivering some specific thing to some specific place, in the way that the milkman delivers milk to your front door. Guernsey is delivering something invisible and intangible to someone unspecified.

One of the problems is that the thing that is being delivered – *core levels of effectiveness* – means nothing whatever. Can a level be *core*? What does *effectiveness* mean here? What are *levels of effectiveness*? The more we probe for meaning, the more its prospect seems to recede.

The second part of the sentence is no better. What do local government and *commercial enterprise* do? They *encourage* someone or something to *evaluate* the island's *ability to deliver* something *in a competitive context*. The whole sentence amounts to saying nothing at all: the island is proud of something unspecified, and the local government and companies encourage something else unspecified. With the benefit of some lateral thinking, and having read the rest of the document, my best guess at what it might mean is this:

Guernsey is proud of being a good place to do business. Our government and local companies make sure we are more business-friendly than the UK, Europe or the Channel Islands.

If you use vague, unspecific words to describe the action, then you have to give that information later on in the sentence. This automatically makes your sentences longer and more complex than they would have been if you had used the right word straight away.

Most sentences have three parts. The first tells you what the subject is, the second tells you what the subject did, and the third supplies the rest of the information – whom the action affected, when, where, and so on. These three parts of the sentence are often called subject, verb and complement. In good sentences, each of these parts is short and clear. If the second part of the sentence (the verb) is a weak word like *undertake*, then the information that should go there (what the subject did) is pushed into the third part of the sentence, where it is liable to get lost.

In each of the following examples, I've highlighted the action words to show how we can make them more specific, providing information earlier on in the sentence:

1. There **is ongoing work** to ensure that we **operate in compliance** with all appropriate codes of corporate governance.

   We **are working** to ensure that we **comply** with all the appropriate codes of corporate governance.

2. You **were given the wrong information**.

   We **misinformed** you.

3. I **am apologetic** in respect of these issues.

   I **apologize** for our mistakes.

4. If you **are agreeable** to this course of action, I **would suggest that you establish contact** with us at your earliest convenience.

   If you **agree**, please **contact** us as soon as you can.

5. Innovation **has been a stimulus** for growth.

   Innovation **has stimulated** growth.

6. The new strategy **has produced improvements** in our levels of efficiency.

   The new strategy **has improved** our efficiency.

The most common of these empty words that delay the point of the sentence are these:

1. to be (am, is, are, was, have been, will be, etc.)

2. to deliver

3. to produce

4. to undertake

5. to carry out

You should also avoid using the words *would*, *could* and *can* wherever possible. They can often simply be deleted, to make the sentence sound more honest and direct:

1. I **would apologize** for this inexcusable delay.

   I **apologize** for this inexcusable delay.

2. I **can guarantee** that you will receive a replacement within three days.

   I **guarantee** that you will receive a replacement within three days.

These words also tend to attract other useless phrases:

I **would point out that** we **have done** everything possible to help you.
We **have done** everything possible to help you.

The point of all of this is to make your writing more active. Basically, it means never using a noun when you can use a verb:

1. **Issuance** of the certificate by Acme took in excess of two years from the initiation of the **application**.

Acme **issued** the certificate more than two years after we **applied** for it.

2. Traditionally, **exploration licensing** in Peru has suffered from a history of poor exploration drilling results, **expropriations** and forced contract **renegotiation**.

Oil companies have **explored** very little in Peru because their drilling has yielded poor results, they have been **expropriated** and their contracts forcibly **renegotiated**.

Using the wrong word for the job

The most straightforward kind of mistake is using the wrong word:

Beverley should have properly **appraised** me of the situation prior to our meeting.

This should read:

Beverley should have properly **apprised** me of the situation prior to our meeting.

There is only an 'a' different, but it completely changes the meaning of the word. To appraise something is to evaluate it. Here the writer was looking for the word *apprise*, which means 'inform'. There are three very simple lessons here:

- Don't use a word unless you are absolutely sure what it means.
- Use a dictionary to check words you're not absolutely sure of – if you find yourself looking up the same

ones over and over again, then write the definition on a post-it note and stick it to your monitor.
- Choose simple words that everyone understands.

The example above would be much more straight-forward as:

Beverley should have told me what was going on before our meeting.

However, there are many completely straightfor-ward words that people often confuse:

Our profits this year have been badly **effected** by the slump in the housing market.

This should read:

Our profits this year have been badly **affected** by the slump in the housing market.

As a verb, *effect* means 'do' or 'put into practice', while *affect* means 'influence'. Because of this confusion, many people instead use the word *impact* as a verb, to mean 'have an impact on' or just 'have an effect on'. This use is not in dictionaries, and many people (including me) think it is ugly. It is much better just to learn the difference between *affect* and *effect*, listed – along with other frequently confused words – in Chapter 15.

Unnecessary, new or made-up words

Sometimes, it isn't clear what is happening in a sen-tence because the writer has used a new term that most people don't understand. In a proposal meeting recently, I heard someone say:

The competition is seen as much stronger in the energy industry, so we'll have to credentialize ourselves in that sector.

What he meant was we would have to emphasize our credentials in the energy industry: say which clients we had worked for, what we had done, which offices specialized in it, and so on. I haven't seen this word written down yet, but I think it's only a matter of time.

Taking a noun and turning it into a verb by adding 'ize' to the end is an increasingly common trend. Here are a few I've heard recently:

- Credentialize – to present your credentials in a particular industry or discipline
- Incentivize – to give someone an incentive
- Optimize – to make something optimal
- Strategize – to formulate a strategy
- Synergize – to bring two things together to create something which is worth more than the sum of both parts
- Utilize – to turn something into a tool, or, in other words, to *use* it
- Actualize – to make something actual, or real
- Conceptualize – to turn something into a concept, or to think of something in a certain way
- Operationalize – to make operational

If any of these words are common in your company, and if everyone knows just what you mean by them, then there's no reason (except taste) why you shouldn't use them in internal documents. Some of them are useful in certain spheres. In IT, *optimizing code* means 'removing unnecessary instructions to make a program run in the most efficient way'. And the word *incentivize* carries the connotation of setting up a system of incentives to make sure that a particular group of people work in a particular way. But either of these can be used too vaguely (*optimize the recruitment process* means 'to make it better', but doesn't say how) or too narrowly (so that *incentivize staff* just means 'paying' them, rather than encompassing other, more personal or social, incentives).

But in any case, all of these words are too new and unfamiliar for a general audience, and their meaning hasn't had time to settle down enough for them to be used with any confidence that your reader will know precisely what you mean. Use them, if you must, in internal documents when you are sure your readers will understand them in precisely the same way you do. But it's best not to use them with other companies, with clients and especially with the public.

This kind of newly minted verb is part of a larger trend. Increasingly, words are used in large corporations in a completely different way to how they are used in any other walk of life. Take a look at this example:

New products such as Kit Kat Kubes, White Maltesers, the new-look Cadbury's CDM range and Mars Galaxy are set to drive chocolate sales.

What does the word *drive* mean here? The standard meanings of the word *drive* are 'to urge in some direction, to force, to direct or to hit'. None of these meanings really apply here. What the writer really means is that those products are going to be the biggest sellers and that because of them the overall sales of chocolate will rise. But it is difficult to tell, because the writer has used a word that can't give any of those useful and specific meanings.

Think hard about what you mean, and use words that convey precisely that meaning. In a recent survey by Office Angels, an employment agency, one in five respondents admitted to using buzzwords that they didn't understand, but I think the real figure must be much higher. Their use and misuse is so common that, to make boring, incomprehensible meetings bearable, people play Buzzword Bingo. Two or three colleagues sneak bingo cards into the meeting, but, instead of numbers, the squares of each card contain buzzwords, such as *deliverable*, *core competency*, *synergy* or *win-win*. Each time someone uses one of the words in the meeting, you cross it off your card, and the first person to get a full house wins.

Summary

- The action should come immediately after the subject. It must be strong, specific and direct.
- Don't make readers wait till the end of the sentence for the action: don't *effect the undertaking of writing*, just *write*.
- Never use a noun when you can verb.
- Don't use a word unless you are absolutely sure what it means.
- Use a dictionary to check words you're not absolutely sure of.

- Choose simple words that everyone understands.
- Before you use a word ending in 'ize', ask yourself whether its meaning is generally understood. Better still, ask someone from outside your company and industry.
- If you're not sure whether something is a buzzword, buy a copy of *The Economist* and try to find it in there. If you can, it's not a buzzword.
- Avoid unspecific and overused words like *drive* and *deliver*. See Chapter 15 for other words to avoid.
- Never put a well-known expression in quotation marks – it just draws attention to the lack of originality.
- If you're not sure whether something is a cliché, check it at www.clichesite.com.

10
Getting the Tone Right

When I talk about the tone of a piece of writing, I just mean the way it sounds – the impression you get of the person who wrote it, and how that makes you feel about them and their opinions. Writing can sound reasonable and authoritative, shrill and overblown, or officious and unconfident. Which you end up with depends on the words you choose and how you use them.

A great brand is just like a great piece of poetry – you know it when you see it. You feel it in your very soul. If I were to show you an IBM logo you would pretty quickly tell me that is a strong brand, if I were to show you an Enron logo you would tell me that is a weak brand.

In this example there is nothing wrong with the sentences – they are direct and clear. But, by claiming in an article written for a general audience that you feel a great brand *in your very soul*, the writer has gone over the top. At that point, he probably lost pretty nearly all of his readers – at least, as soon as they realized that he wasn't being satirical. Any readers who swallowed the comparison of brands to poetry and didn't demur when the writer claimed to feel them in his *very soul* (the word *very* here is particularly off-putting – no one could say it with a straight face) must have noticed how poor the examples were. Enron was one of the strongest brands in the world until everyone found out about its criminal dishonesty. And IBM makes perfectly good computers, but it is a notably unpoetic company.

To make the writer's point – that people have a strong and immediate reaction to brands – to a general audience, we need to approach it in a completely different way. Most people do not like to think of themselves as slaves to brands, so using the word *you* is probably not a good idea. Also most people flatter themselves that their most deep and spiritual feelings are not susceptible to manipulation by marketing men and publicity experts. To sell the point, we need to talk about other people, and we need a good, concrete example that cannot be challenged:

People's response to brands is surprisingly strong and immediate. In blind taste tests, people prefer Pepsi; but when they know which sample is which, Coke comes out on top every time. We clearly have a gut reaction to strong brands.

The three most common ways of getting the tone of a piece of writing wrong are:

- Going over the top – especially in sales pitches
- Sounding officious and evasive – especially in responding to complaints
- Sounding timid and uncertain – especially in reports and when making recommendations

Sales pitches – the limits of enthusiasm

It's often important to be positive about your products and your services, but do you sound a little breathless?

Dear Friend,

Congratulations on your new business venture! Your company has been specially selected to test the GALLERY PEN, one of our most popular products. A sample of the GALLERY PEN, inscribed with your name and address, is enclosed for your inspection. This **personalized FREE sample** is yours to keep.

Obviously, we cannot make a FREE gift of this kind to everyone, but have chosen you because your opinion is very important to us. Notice the GALLERY PEN's exceptional writing quality and distinctive design. The colourful top, easy-to-handle body and long-lasting ink capacity make the GALLERY PEN a writing instrument which you will be proud to give to your friends and business clients. Each time they use it, your company will be remembered. Is there any better way to advertise or to keep your name in front of your customers?

Again, in this example the sentences are not grammatically wrong, but the tone they convey is insincere. It is important to sound friendly and positive, but the way to do this is not to address a stranger as *Dear Friend* – it sounds false, as does telling me that I have been *specially selected*. In this case, I know I haven't been specially selected: I got this letter because I have somehow got onto a junk mailing list as a new company. I recently had a phone call from a sales rep asking to speak to 'the owner or manager of Chris Shevlin'.

But even if I didn't know that I'd received this in error, even if I were the owner of a new business venture, I would still be put off by the patronizing insincerity and the repeated BLOCK CAPITALS emphasizing that I have been given a FREE pen, the name of which is repeated over and over again. Perhaps I am jaded, but I no longer find much cause for excitement in a free pen. The problem continues in the second paragraph: the company clearly can make a FREE gift of this kind to everyone on its mailing list, and I have no idea why my opinion is very important to them.

It is impossible to make something impressive just by shouting excitedly about it, and glowing descriptions of things tend to amuse rather than impress. When you sound over-enthusiastic, people stop believing you. Although it's important to be positive about your company, and its products and services, you can alienate people if you step over the bounds of credibility.

Aim instead to sound measured and genuine, and to convince with facts rather than rhetoric. Be respectful, but not fawning: the way to address a sales letter is *Dear Mr Shevlin*, not *Dear Friend* or – worse – *Dear Valued Customer*. You demonstrate friendliness by being respectful and considering your prospective client's interests, not by simply calling them *Friend*. You demonstrate that you value your customers in the same way. That means not telling me transparent untruths about how I've been specially selected, and how valuable my opinion is, but telling me how and why I might benefit by having your products. Tell me what other customers have said about the benefits, and tell me, if you can, about research that has been done, or what a respected commentator has said.

Dear Mr Shevlin,

When starting up a new business, the little things can make all the difference. I have enclosed a sample of one of our pens, personalized for you, because our clients tell us that they help. Geoffrey Rayne, who owns a small cycle-import business in Winchester, wrote to me to say:

> *'I was surprised how much difference your pens made to the perception of our company. Although it's a simple thing, staff and customers have told me that having our own branded pens adds to the feeling that we are a strong and successful company.'*

And in a recent article, *Business Week* rated branded merchandise one of the most cost-effective methods of marketing a new business . . .

Be respectful, give people the facts, don't patronize, and never try to sell something with an exclamation mark. The best salespeople aren't the ones who work themselves up into a lather, but the ones who politely allow the customer to convince himself.

To ensure that you don't stray into off-putting breathlessness, check your writing for these things:

- Excessive enthusiasm. Don't try to sell with an exclamation mark. Rather than trying to interest your
customer by describing things in an over-excited
way, focus on the benefits. Show, don't tell. Look at
each exclamation mark and ask yourself: 'Does this
tell the customer something useful, or am I just
trying to show how excited I am?'
- Insincerity. Don't say things that neither you nor the
customer believe. Check for things such as saying
Dear Friend to someone you've never met. And
delete unnecessary qualifiers: *as a* valued *customer*,
your good self, *this* unparalleled *offer*. The more you
give it to people straight, the more they are likely to
accept what you say.

Answering complaints – don't be evasive or impersonal

Although you don't want to sound too informal, it is
important that people get the sense that you are a
real person. Officious language prevents any rapport
between you and your readers, and it often makes you
sound as though you are trying to avoid responsibility
for your mistakes.

I am now in receipt of your letter of 24 May 2004 from
which I was disappointed to learn of your difficulties.

Having investigated your concern, the information
you were given regarding the offer of free flights
when paying for your accommodation by debit card
was wrong. This benefit was available to specific

existing customers, but was not available to new customers. As a tangible gesture of regret, I have made arrangements to send you a gift which I hope you will accept in the spirit it is intended.

I trust this resolves matters to your satisfaction. Thank you for taking the time and trouble to bring this matter to my attention.

I have never heard anyone say *I am in receipt of* – it is only ever written, and it is only ever found in the driest and most tedious writing. The straightforward way of saying this is simply *I have received your letter*. The polite way is to say *Thank you for your letter*.

By using the phrase *I was disappointed to learn of your difficulties*, the writer sounds disapproving of the reader, and implies that the complaint is the reader's own fault. It is always possible to say *I am sorry to hear that* or simply *I am sorry that*. The words *I am sorry* can be an expression of sympathy, and do not have to imply that you are admitting fault.

An introduction that begins with an *-ing* word should apply to the subject that follows. In the second paragraph of this example, the information hasn't investigated anyone's concern. The person who investigated was the writer, so *having investigated your concern* should be followed by *I*.

When you begin a sentence with a short description, such as *Having investigated* or *As a long-standing customer*, the very next thing you mention should be the thing to which this description applies. If you start a sentence with *Based on the average price*, you should say what is based on that price. If you start one with *Having secured control*, you should follow it with the person or organization that has secured control.

- *Having investigated your concern*, I . . .' because it was *I* who investigated the concern.
- *As a long-standing customer*, you . . .' because *you* are the long-standing customer.

In the second sentence of the sample letter, the writer does not clearly state whose fault it was that the customer was misinformed. If the company is writing the letter, it is much better to take responsibility and say *I'm sorry that we misinformed you about* . . . Saying things indirectly doesn't lessen the mistake, it just makes you look evasive.

Anything that increases the appearance that you are taking action is a good thing. Rather than *I have made arrangements to send a gift*, it is better to say *I will send you a gift*. Similarly, it is better to avoid the connotations of insincerity that the word *gesture* has (as in 'gesture politics') and be more direct; *to show we regret what has happened* or, more simply still, *to say sorry for our mistakes* are better ways of introducing the gift.

It is also worth remembering that, by denying or dismissing something, you may give it more force. The salesman who litters his speech with phrases like *I'll be honest* or *to tell you the truth* makes himself seem less, not more, trustworthy. Why would he need to say this unless his honesty were somehow in question? The same applies in the second paragraph of this letter: the writer says that she hopes the gift will be *accepted in the spirit intended*, but the only reason for saying this is that she fears the gift will not be accepted in this way. By raising this possibility, she makes the response she fears more likely.

The final paragraph sounds like a stock phrase. This makes the letter seem more impersonal, and implies that not much investigation went on. It is also presumptuous to *trust* that the reply satisfies the customer: if it does, there is no need to say it; if it doesn't, saying this will annoy the customer more.

The last sentence implies that the customer only complained as a matter of courtesy. If the customer is angry or frustrated – as is often the case when people complain – a sentence like this is likely to annoy them more, as it seems to trivialize the complaint.

In general, it is better to say nothing than to use standard paragraphs. Begin by thanking the customer for their letter, sympathize with their specific complaint and then go straight into an explanation of its cause. End by inviting the customer to get in touch if you haven't explained anything properly. The explanation is the main thing, and the more thoroughly you seem to explain, the happier your customer will be.

Thank you for your letter of 24 May. I am very sorry to hear that we misinformed you about our free flights offer.

I apologize that our sales assistant told you that your debit-card payment for accommodation was included in the offer. In fact, the offer is only available to existing customers paying by credit card.

I asked the sales assistant, Carina Beaumont, how she came to make the mistake, and she tells me that she misread the information she was given. She is usually very conscientious, and she asked me to pass on her apologies. I'm confident that she won't make the same mistake again. To show how sorry we are, I have sent you a gift, which should reach you in the next few days.

I hope that we won't let ourselves down like this again. In the meantime, if there's anything I could have explained better, please let me know.

When people complain, what they want most of all is a frank apology. The details of that apology are very important to them, as is the feeling that you have read their letter thoroughly and done something about it. Even if there is not much to say, as in the above example, you need to spell out everything you have done to investigate the complaint, and apologize clearly and unreservedly for everything your company has done wrong, however small or accidental.

When answering complaints, aim to sound *human* and *reasonable*. To do this, go through your letter and do the following:

1. Remove anything that you would feel embarrassed or uncomfortable saying to someone if they were in the room.

2. If there is a simpler or more everyday alternative, use it.

3. Simply say what has happened in the most direct, factual and straightforward way you can.

4. Use the words *who*, *we*, and *you* to bring people into your explanation. Give names wherever possible.

5. If you (or your company) have done anything wrong, say what it is and apologize for it. Ideally, do this right at the beginning of the letter – it will disarm your reader straight away.

6. When apologizing, be direct: say *I'm sorry* or *I apologize*, not *it is to be regretted* or *we are apologetic*.

7. Don't be presumptuous.

8. Look out for passives, such as *The payment due on 14 December was not made*. When answering complaints letters, it is important to say who did what, and passive sentences tend to leave the *who* bit out.

Giving recommendations – the importance of confidence

Do you sound unsure of yourself? This is another extract from the Strategic Rail Authority's report:

A strategy that allows time for system development, and the planned synchronization of the fitment of ERTMS to track and train would enable more of System D to be implemented. This is estimated to potentially increase capacity by up to 10% with complementary investment, and would potentially attract passengers from road to rail.

Of course it isn't always possible to be entirely in favour of or opposed to any course of action, but you can explain why, rather than hedging and qualifying with every word, as the last sentence above does. The definite form of the final sentence would be:

This will increase capacity by 10% and will attract passengers from road to rail.

The authors don't want to say anything as categorical as that, but they certainly don't need all of the qualifiers they use. Here is that sentence again with all the words that negate, mitigate or temporize indicated in brackets:

This (*is estimated to*) (*potentially*) increase capacity by (*up to*) 10% (*with complementary investment*), and (*would*) (*potentially*) attract passengers from road to rail.

That's six qualifiers in a 23-word sentence. Or perhaps I should say: that is estimated to be potentially up to six qualifiers in what would appear to be a sentence of up to 23 words. We get the message that this is not a cast-iron guarantee after the first qualifier, so what are the others doing there? They are making the sentence harder to understand and undercutting any authority the writer might have had.

The writers begin by saying *this is estimated to*, but they do not say *who* has estimated this. That immediately makes the sentence less direct, quantifiable and easy to grasp. An estimate is, by its very nature, inexact, so the word *potentially* adds nothing – it just signals to the reader not to accord any credence to any of the vague hints the writers may give. The 10% figure, which the writers have already told us is approximate, is further weakened with the qualifier *up to*, and the whole thing is made to depend on *complementary investment*, which isn't explained – money from some-where else to be spent on something else.

The vague and uncertain prospect which would attract the passengers has already been qualified almost into oblivion – made so uncertain that the writer is saying almost nothing. Nevertheless, the writer still feels the need to inject a fresh note of uncertainty. In fact, he injects two notes of uncertainty. The word *would* alone shows that what follows is conditional or hypothetical. The word *potentially* shows the same thing, so there is no need for both expressions: they are a tautology.

I am not saying you should never qualify a state-ment, only that you should think about exactly what you are qualifying and why, and say things in the most direct way possible. It is possible to say the same thing as the example above, but more directly – while still clearly showing that nothing is guaranteed:

More of System D could be implemented if ERTMS were fitted to track and trains at the same time, and if time were allowed for the system to be developed. The team of experts from across Europe estimates that, if there were other investment as well, capacity would increase by 10%, attracting passengers from the roads.

If you do need to qualify something, make sure you qualify the right thing, and only that thing. For example:

It is estimated that this may potentially take up to ten years.

In this sentence, if it is only the length of time that is uncertain, then it is much better to say *This will take up to ten years* or *This will take about ten years*. Wherever possible, try to put things into context. *This could take as long as ten years* is even better, because it tells the reader that, in this context, ten years is a long time.

It is always tempting to qualify what we say, to water it down and insure ourselves against being wrong by using expressions like *may*, *potentially*, *in my opinion*, *it is thought that* and so on. The problem is that this is frustrating to read and difficult to grasp. What's more, it sends a powerful message that the reader should place no faith in what you say. It is easy to get into the habit of overusing these expressions. Very often, when you really think about it, you can dispense with them altogether. After all, it is usually obvious when what you write is your opinion. If you tell your readers how you arrived at your conclusions, they will be able to decide for themselves how much credence to give them.

Rather than qualifying everything, aim to sound *confident* and *authoritative*. Make clear statements and support them with evidence.

1. Go through your work, carefully looking for qualifying terms such as *could*, *would*, *potentially*, *might*, *may*, *up to*, *arguably*, *probably*, *possibly*, *in my opinion*, *it is thought that*, *it is estimated that*. Ask yourself whether you need each one.

2. Instead of saying *it is thought that* or *it is estimated that*, say *who* thinks or estimates. If it is you, then own up.

3. Never use two qualifying expressions at once: *would potentially* is redundant. You need only one of the two.

4. Qualify as straightforwardly as possible. Wherever possible, you should explain why what you say is not certain.

5. It is often obvious that what you write is your own opinion, evaluation or estimate, so you do not need to emphasize the fact. Check wherever you say *I think*, *I believe*, *it seems to me* and so on.

Summary

- Don't try to sell with an exclamation mark.
- Don't say things that neither you nor your reader believes.
- Simply say what has happened in the most direct, factual and straightforward way you can.
- If you (or your company) have done anything wrong, say what it is and apologize for it right at the beginning of the letter.
- When apologizing, be direct: say *I'm sorry* or *I apologize*, not *it is to be regretted* or *we are apologetic*.
- Go through your work, carefully looking for qualifying terms such as *could, would, potentially, might, may, up to, arguably, probably, possibly, in my opinion, it is thought that, it is estimated that*. Ask yourself whether you need each one.
- Qualify as straightforwardly as possible. Wherever possible, you should explain why what you say is not certain.
- It is often obvious that what you write is your own opinion, evaluation or estimate, so you do not need to emphasize the fact. Check wherever you say *I think*, *I believe*, *it seems to me*, and so on.

• If, before writing, you read something that has the tone you want, it will help you to achieve that in your own writing. For general business purposes, the *Financial Times* and *The Economist* are excellent.

11
Getting the Length Right

Giant sentences

Here is a 101-word sentence from the annual report of a pharmaceutical company called Shire:

The directors have considered Resolutions 1 to 11 which deal with, inter alia, the proposals relating to authority to make market purchases, to increase borrowing limits, to set up an Employee Benefit Trust and to set up a Deferred Bonus Plan to be put to shareholders and believe they are in the best interests of shareholders as a whole and accordingly recommend that shareholders vote in favour of them at the Annual General Meeting as they intend to do in respect of their aggregated beneficial holdings of 6,791,916 ordinary shares, representing approximately 1.4% of the issued share capital of the Company.

Someone seems to have set out to make it as long and complex as possible, in the process making it extremely difficult to read and understand. Sentences are usually more readable and comprehensible if they have relatively few different parts. The more parts a sentence has, the simpler each one should be.

To make this sentence bearable, we need to break it down into its constituent parts. A good way of doing this is to look for the main actions (or verbs) in the sentence:

- The directors **have considered** Resolutions 1 to 11
- which **deal with**, inter alia, the proposals relating to authority
  - **to make** market purchases,
  - **to increase** borrowing limits,
  - **to set up** an Employee Benefit Trust and
  - **to set up** a Deferred Bonus Plan to be put to shareholders
- and **believe** they are in the best interests of share-holders as a whole
- and accordingly **recommend** that shareholders **vote** in favour of them at the Annual General Meeting
- as they **intend** to do in respect of their aggregated beneficial holdings of 6,791,916 ordinary shares
- **representing** approximately 1.4% of the issued share capital of the Company.

A good sentence has a single, clear subject followed by a specific, concrete action. Just by looking for the actions, we have a pretty good basis for breaking the monster 101-word sentence into manageable components:

The directors **have considered** Resolutions 1 to 11. These resolutions **deal with**, inter alia, the proposals relating to authority **to make** market purchases, **to increase** borrowing limits, **to set up** an Employee Benefit Trust and **to set up** a Deferred Bonus Plan to be put to shareholders. The directors **believe** they are in the best interests of shareholders as a whole. The directors accordingly **recommend** that shareholders **vote** in favour of them at the Annual General Meeting. The directors **intend** to vote this way in respect of their aggregated beneficial holdings of 6,791,916 ordinary shares. These holdings **represent** approximately 1.4% of the issued share capital of the Company.

It is still not great, but at least now we can breathe, and there is less danger of our getting lost amid the giant flabby folds of the original. It would be even better to apply what we learned earlier: to give the essence of the sentence first, and then supply the detailed information. This, and a modicum of translation (I've assumed that the new powers are for the chief executive), allows us to improve a bit more:

The directors have considered the 11 resolutions, and believe they are in shareholders' best interests. Among other things, these resolutions include proposals for giving the chief executive more powers. The powers are to make market purchases, to increase borrowing limits, and to set up an Employee Benefit Trust and a Deferred Bonus Plan. The directors have 6,791,916 ordinary shares between them, representing around 1.4% of the company's issued share capital. They intend to use their shares to vote in favour of the resolutions. They recommend that shareholders do the same.

It is important to remember that there is no tax on sentences. Sentences can be shortened. You can use as many as you like. Make them as short as you like. You won't be charged. To neaten things up so that we don't repeat subjects too often, we might decide to amalgamate a couple of the sentences:

The directors have considered the 11 resolutions, and believe they are in shareholders' best interests. Among other things, these resolutions include proposals for giving the chief executive powers to make market purchases, increase borrowing limits, and set up an Employee Benefit Trust and a Deferred Bonus Plan. The directors have 6,791,916 ordinary shares between them, representing around 1.4% of the company's issued share capital. They intend to use their shares to vote in favour of the resolutions, and recommend that shareholders do the same.

This reduces our single, 101-word sentence to an 84-word paragraph of four sentences, with an average length of 21 words. That is a good average to aim for.

Pretty much every piece of advice ever given about writing includes some variation on the so-called 'KISS principle': Keep It Short and Simple – or the more brutal Keep It Simple, Stupid. There are two problems with this advice. Firstly, it is all very well telling people to keep it simple, but it is very difficult to tell them how. Secondly, people often seem to dislike the idea of writing simply. An American I met recently summed it up with the words, 'I like wordy, goddammit.' Writing in a complicated way seems to make people feel like 'proper' writers.

Yet if you look at the way 'proper' writers (authors, novelists, journalists) write, their sentences are very rarely complex, complicated or wordy. But nor does their writing feel simplistic – at least not with the connotations of being rudimentary or foolish. Their writing feels natural, articulate, grown-up, fluid – but not usually simplistic.

It strikes me that what we really mean when we say keep it simple (stupid) is 'keep it under control'. Controlled, structured sentences – long or short, simple or complex – are easier for readers to understand. Ease of understanding is important when writing at work, where we can guess that most of our readers won't be reading our report, letter or email while curled up on the sofa with a nice glass of red wine.

In fact, you can take it for granted that most of your readers will be stressed, tired and pushed for time. To get through to these people, you need to do their work for them. You need to pre-digest what they're reading, so that they aren't left with anything to figure out. That means making your sentences direct, comprehensible and well-structured. They don't necessarily have to be short, but long sentences are more likely to be confusing than short ones simply because there is more scope for error. You can pack more clauses and sub-clauses into a long sentence, add more long strings of adjectives to your abstract nouns, and separate the verb from its subject by a greater distance. But it is these things that make the sentence difficult, not its mere length.

If you want to use longer sentences, then you need to be able to do short, direct sentences, because good long sentences are made up of the same elements as good short ones. If you can see all kinds of writing as being elaborations on a solid underlying structure, then you can control your writing better. This gives you much more freedom and flexibility. In the example above, we broke things down so that there was a single action in each sentence, and then decided that a couple of them could be amalgamated to keep the paragraph flowing.

Sentences within sentences

Many people's problems with sentences arise because they try to make them do too much. Ideally, a sentence should communicate just one idea – or two, if one leads naturally into the other.

Always ask yourself:

- Is this sentence trying to do too much?
- Can I break this sentence up?

Sentences often get out of control because the writer keeps adding extra detail to the sentence he has, rather than rethinking and restructuring. That is what has happened to this sentence:

This course is all about developing a credible response to any potential threat to IT services that may result in business interruption that is efficient, effective and aligned to business requirements.

You probably had to read that at least a couple of times to work out what the writer meant to say. At first glance, he seems to be saying that IT services may result in business interruption, and that business interruption is efficient, effective and aligned to business requirements.

This mistake arises because the writer thinks that *potential threat to IT services* will be read as the subject of the first *that* – i.e. it is the potential threat that 'may result in business interruption'. He then thinks that *a credible response to any potential threat to IT services that may result in business interruption* will be read as the subject of the second *that* – i.e. it is the credible response that is 'efficient, effective and aligned to business requirements'.

But readers don't hold such huge structures in their heads very well, and where there is a choice of things for a construction to modify, we tend to choose the simple one immediately before it. Readers can work it all out if they put in the time and effort, but the writer could have made it easy for them.

The extra details that overwhelm a sentence are often added by means of linking words, such as *that*, *which*, *for*, *and*, *but*, *of*, *because*, *by* and *if*. In this case, the linking words are not beside the words to which they refer. Unfortunately, changing this sentence to put them there would just push apart bits of structure that need to be together:

This course is all about developing a credible response that is efficient, effective and aligned to business requirements to any potential threat that may result in business interruption to IT services.

We could use brackets to make it more comprehensible, but it looks messy and it still isn't readable:

This course is all about developing a credible response (that is efficient, effective and aligned to business requirements) to any potential threat (that may result in business interruption) to IT services.

The only real option is to break the links which add extra detail and move the detail into separate sentences:

This course is all about developing a credible response to any potential threat to IT services. The response must focus on threats that could result in business interruption, and it must be efficient, effective and aligned to business requirements.

Again, what we are doing is stating the most essential point first – the summary – and then adding detail by taking the things we mentioned in the summary, making them the subject of their own sentences and supplying extra information.

Overgrown sentences

Sometimes detail gradually accumulates in different drafts, until the sentence gets swamped and choked up with extra words. Often, the structure would have worked if things had been kept simple, but the different elements of the sentence grow out of control – like plants in a neglected formal garden. Through the towering weeds, we can dimly see the outlines of lawn and flowerbed:

Despite the present environment of deep uncertainty surrounding the situations in Iraq and Venezuela and the fact that the agreement was reached in mid January 2003 to raise OPEC ceiling production by a further 1.5 million b/d to offset a supply shortage and reduce prices, Algeria's overproduction was at its highest ever level.

The basic structure is sound:

Despite *this* and *this*, this *happened*.

Perhaps originally it read like this:

Despite Iraq and the OPEC agreement, Algeria's overproduction was at its highest ever level.

Put this way, it is pretty straightforward. Algeria has produced too much oil even though there are two very good reasons not to. However, those two reasons have become too detailed to fit comfortably into the sentence's structure. In the original version, by the time we get to Algeria's overproduction, we have forgotten the word *despite*. The reader is asked to carry too much in his head. Very often, with structures like this, we can swap the elements around:

Algeria's overproduction was at its highest ever level, despite the present environment of deep uncertainty surrounding the situations in Iraq and Venezuela and the fact that the agreement was reached in mid January 2003 to raise OPEC ceiling production by a further 1.5 million b/d to offset a supply shortage and reduce prices.

This still isn't great, but the reader no longer has to carry so much in his head.

At 53 words, this is still a very long sentence, and too involved to be easily understood. We can reduce the length a little bit by finding more straightforward ways of saying things. *The present environment of deep uncertainty surrounding the situations in* doesn't say anything more than *the deep uncertainty about*. The word *environment* – like *situation* – can often be cut out. *Present* is also frequently a wasted word, since readers will always assume you are talking about the present unless there is a good reason for them not to.

But while we can save six words here, the bit about OPEC is far longer and more complex. When something is complex, it is always a good idea to give it its own sentence. Again, we are following our standard strategy of stating the basic message and then supplying more detail. The second sentence echoes the structure of the first. But, since we already know that Algeria overproduced despite something, the second sentence refers back to this overproduction and acknowledges the repetition of the word *despite* with the word *also*.

Algeria overproduced by a record amount, despite the deep uncertainty about Iraq and Venezuela. This overproduction also came despite OPEC's agreement in January 2003 to raise its production ceiling – by another 1.5 million b/d (barrels per day) – in order to reduce prices and offset the supply shortage.

The second sentence is still rather long, but we keep it moving by adding one piece of detail between dashes. We could decide to split the second sentence into two, but I think it makes it flow less well. What do you think?

Algeria overproduced by a record amount, despite the deep uncertainty about Iraq and Venezuela. Its overproduction also came despite OPEC's agreement, in January 2003, to raise its production ceiling. In order to reduce prices and offset the supply shortage, the ceiling will increase by 1.5 million b/d (barrels per day).

Stunted sentences

A comfortable average length for sentences is between 20 and 25 words. Occasionally one of your sentences will be slightly more than 30 words long, and occasionally one will be very short. Although I said before to make sentences as short as you like, if you use too many very short sentences one after another, your writing will become staccato and difficult to read. Lots of very short sentences together can sound rather like barking:

Acme project. New application feedback received from Acme. Ongoing. Progressed to phase of working with Accreditation Section. Given documentation to the section. The section has responded. Responded to section with clarification.

The writer of this example has composed it like a computer issuing responses to a series of commands. The subject of the paragraph is given in a separate sentence of its own at the beginning, followed by a series of bulletins. Although all the facts are there, they are difficult to take in because we don't know how they relate to one another, and many of the cues and linking words that help guide the reader's attention are missing.

With passages like this example, the first thing to do is to make sure we are dealing with full sentences. To do this we:

- Ensure that every sentence has a verb, so that the reader knows what is happening.

- Add in missing words such as *our*, *the*, *a* and *some*. These help to introduce the objects you mention, and they make sentences sound fully formed.

Doing this to our original example immediately makes it easier to understand:

We have an Acme project. We have received new feedback about our application from Acme. The feedback is ongoing. The application has progressed to the phase of working with Acme's Accreditation Section. We have given documentation to the section. The section has responded. We have responded to the section with clarification.

The second thing to do is to ensure a smooth flow of information. To do this we:

- Avoid repeating the subject by using words such as *and* and *which* to link sentences together: 'We have given . . . *and* have responded' or 'our application, *which* has now . . .'.
- Add comment and context, saying how things are going, when they happened and whether they are increasing or decreasing. Express relationships between sentences by using words such as *later*, *however*, *unfortunately*, *despite*, *after* and *because of*.

The way to make short sentences flow is to show how they relate to one another, and to include comment and context with the bare facts:

Our Acme project is going well. We are still getting feedback from Acme about our application, which has now progressed to the stage of working with their Accreditation Section. We have given the section the documentation they asked for, and have responded to their request for some of it to be clarified.

Very short sentences only become a problem if there are lots of them, one after another. Used well, they can add emphasis to a point. This one comes after three relatively long paragraphs in Accenture's report, *The Innovator's Advantage*:

The conclusion is clear. In volatile times, innovation remains a springboard to survival and prosperity. And the approaches to business outlined here, especially in relation to the management of IT, provide a key to unlock the true potential value of the organization.

In this example, the short sentence works well to give the paragraph rhythm and to signal that we have reached an important point. Note that the third sentence begins with *and*. Beginning a sentence with *and* or *but* is perfectly fine if you want to add a rhetorical touch. But make sure the point warrants it, and that you really do want to add something important (*and*) or show a significant contrast (*but*).

Bullet-points

Is your writing riddled with bullets? If any one page has more than five bullet-points, then you are probably being too trigger-happy. There are times when the style demands that you use more bullet-points – as in a table of contents or a technical manual's list of features – but in standard business writing, five to a page is about your limit. Bullets are useful when they draw attention to important points: key questions, significant facts or essential concepts. When there are two or three things your reader just *has* to know, bullets are ideal.

Before you call the IT department, please do the following:
- Save your work
- Check that your computer is plugged in
- Restart your computer

Or:

Our work falls into three categories:
- Research – we conduct nationwide consumer surveys
- Publishing – we produce *Outlook*, a bimonthly magazine
- Consulting – we advise companies on consumer trends and attitudes

But if you find yourself using bullets more than that, the chances are that they will confuse your reader. The problem is that bullets aren't much good at showing relationships between things. They are lists; and, in general, the more items there are in a list, the looser the relationship between them. In excess, they also fatigue your reader because they are inherently monotonous – good for computers to process, bad for people, who need rhythm and variety.

The writer of the following example has definitely used too many lists and too many bullets. In the course of a single article – intended to promote his HR company – he used 34 bullet-points. In fact, the words in his bullet-points outnumbered those in the text. While bullet-points are good for drawing attention to things, if you try to draw attention to everything, you will produce the opposite effect.

A group of 15 people were taken from their day jobs to manage the initial stages of our change programme, i.e. overseeing and supporting the 11 pilots which were established. They covered a wide range of activities:

- A web-based new core administration system
- Workflow and imaging software
- New ways of working based on process teams
- Institute of Customer Service (ICS) Awards Programme
- New ways of working, between our consulting and pension administration teams
- Creating an electronic scheme knowledge base for each scheme administered
- Standardizing and automating the production of letters and reports
- Changing procedures for checking of work
- Improvements in our pensioner payroll facility
- Electronic reconciliation of standard information from the Department of Work and Pensions (DWP)
- Ensuring all scheme membership data is complete and reconciled.

Eleven points is far too many, especially when they are so diverse and none of them is self-explanatory. A list like this is indigestible – there is no way for the reader to learn anything useful from it. To make it digestible, you have to consider what you want your reader to take from it. What does the list mean? To answer that, you have to look for similarities and differences between the items in the list. Grouping things together gives you an easy way of introducing them, and the differences between the groups make it easy to move from one subject to another.

In this example, the real solution was to ask the writer why he was giving the reader such a lot of long lists – to ask what he wanted to communicate. However, it is possible just to present the information above in a more engaging way. To turn bullet-points into text, look for the similarities and differences between them, and put them into groups. Then begin your writing by introducing the groups. This will help you to build a narrative that includes the contents of each bullet:

A team of 15 were taken from their day jobs to work full-time on the change programme. To get things going, they launched 11 pilot projects, focusing on pioneering new ways of working, installing new IT systems and overhauling the way we check our work. New ways of working meant setting up a dedicated team for each process, and co-ordinating our consulting and pension administration teams. To get people committed to these new ways of working, we joined the Institute of Customer Service (ICS) Awards Programme, giving our people a goal to work towards.

On the IT front, we built a new web-based administration system to hold all our knowledge of each scheme we administer – with a separate project to check this knowledge. Along with workflow and imaging software, this new system will allow us to automatically incorporate all the information sent to us by the Department of Work and Pensions (DWP). It will also enable us to standardize and automate our production of letters and reports, and support improvements in our pensioner payroll facility.

On the other hand, sometimes the reverse is needed. If a piece of writing is looking too dense and unapproachable, bullet-points are a good way of making it seem more accessible – as well as highlighting particular points. If you have some hard-hitting facts, but are struggling to integrate them into a flowing paragraph, bullet-points can be the solution.

Our research identified a range of damaging impacts on the millions of families who have little choice but to use this form of credit to help make ends meet. For instance there is little evidence of switching by home credit customers – either between home credit companies or to other credit providers; it is expensive – with average interest rates of 177 per cent – which means the poorest pay more for their loans; and a small number of companies dominate the market, which means high market concentration and limited competition.

This has much more impact as bullet-points:

Millions of families have little choice but to use home credit to make ends meet, but our research identified three big problems with the market:
- High cost – the average interest rate is 177 per cent
- Inadequate competition – five companies dominate the market
- Inadequate choice – few customers change providers

Using bullet-points here makes the issues more apparent, and avoids the very long sentence beginning *For instance*. Notice that every bullet begins with a two-word, adjective-noun summary, and that each sets out a problem with the market. It is very easy to forget to keep bullet-points consistent:

This year we have:
- Launched our new product, ActiveWire
- Installed a new customer relationship management system
- Our marketing campaign has generated considerable awareness among targeted customers

The first two items begin with past-tense verbs and complete the sentence beginning *This year we have*. But in the final item, the writer has forgotten about the introduction and just given a full sentence. To fit, it should read:

- Run a marketing campaign that has generated considerable awareness among targeted customers

Begin each bullet-point with the same kind of words, so that every one of them fits the sentence that introduces them.

Punctuation

Sometimes sentences overrun simply because we forget to put in the full stop. However, various punctuation marks can be useful for splitting your sentences up into manageable chunks and indicating how the different parts fit together. The most important are:

- Colons – for introducing lists, bullet-points and explanations
- Commas – for indicating comments, clauses and pauses
- Full stops – for splitting up overlong sentences
- Dashes – for explaining while keeping your writing moving

These, and all the other main punctuation marks, are dealt with in Chapter 13.

Summary

- There's more scope for confusion and mistakes in long sentences, so if a sentence is much over 30 words, it will almost certainly need attention.
- To break up a long sentence, look for the actions. Give each main action its own sentence.
- An average sentence length of 20 to 25 words is comfortable – to read and write.
- Don't keep packing extra words into the sentences you have: form new sentences.
- Always ask yourself:
  - Is this sentence trying to do too much?
  - Can I break this sentence up?
- Look at words like *that, which, for, and, but, of, because, by* and *if*. They often show detail that can be moved into separate sentences.
- When using sentences that rely heavily on structure, keep each part simple. In a sentence like 'Despite *this* and *this*, *this* happened' or 'If *this*, then *this*', each *this* should be as short and simple as possible.
- Try to avoid having lots of very short sentences (eight words or fewer) one after another.
- Make sure you are writing in full sentences. Each one needs a verb, and words such as *this, our, the, a* and *some* are valuable, not optional.
- Add comment and context by using words such as *later, however, unfortunately, despite, after* and *because of*.

- Use bullet-points to highlight two to four things that your reader just *has* to know.
- To turn bullet-points into text, group them and then describe those groups.
- Keep every bullet in a list consistent. Make sure every one of them agrees with the sentence that introduces them.

Part 3

The Details: Checking

Now all that remains is for you to check your work thoroughly, making sure no detail will let it down.

12
Tools for Checking

When it comes to making sure that your writing is correct, there are a number of different tools you can call on: dictionaries, thesauruses, and guides to grammar, usage and style. I recommend that you get hold of a dictionary and a style guide. This does not necessarily mean spending money, since there are a number of good resources available free on the Internet. In this chapter, I suggest how to use each of these different tools, with both print and Internet versions of each. I then recommend two other editing tools that are often overlooked: your voice, and the editing marks you use.

Dictionaries

Recommendations

• *The Penguin Dictionary*, by Robert Allen, 2004

A decent dictionary is well worth the money, and will last a long time. Even a pocket dictionary is better than nothing, but if you have the space and the autonomy at work then a proper breeze-block sized dictionary is essential. The most obvious use for a dictionary is to look up words that you don't know, but it is often even more useful to look up words that you *think* you already know. We often pick up words from reading and make assumptions about their meanings from the context in which we first find them. Sometimes we get the meaning exactly right, but more often we miss out some nuance – or even get the wrong end of the stick altogether.

If you write with a dictionary beside you, you can look up any word that you use – even when you're almost sure you know it. Being able to check that you are right is a great way of getting more confident with words. I recommend Penguin's dictionary partly because it includes 'usage notes' that tell you how to use the words that most often trip people up. It also tells you where words come from, with word histories for some of the more useful or interesting examples. Knowing where a word came from often gives you a firmer grasp of its meaning.

Dictionaries are also very good for general reference. If something you are reading mentions Zen Buddhism or the first law of thermodynamics, it can be very handy to be able to look up a brief description that tells you – in a couple of sentences – all you need to know in order to read on. They are also a good way of reminding yourself of what abbreviations such as TGWU or SWOT stand for.

If you don't have the desk-space, or if you do a lot of travelling, you might prefer to use a dictionary on your computer. If you don't want to buy one on

CD-ROM, there are some available on the Internet. As with everything on the web, sites and addresses can change rapidly, but at the time of writing WordIQ.com and Dictionary.com are both pretty good – and WordIQ also includes a very good thesaurus. The problem is that they use American spellings, and it can be difficult to find the British versions, which is why it's better to use a paper dictionary if you can.

Uses
- Looking up words that aren't in your computer's spelling checker
- Getting advice about the best ways to use words
- Answering general reference questions, such as finding out what the difference is between ozone and oxygen, or checking what a Visigoth is
- Looking at the different ways you can use a word: for example, whether the adjective and adverb forms of a word are different, as with *quick* and *quickly*, or the same, as with *fast*
- Finding out how to pronounce unusual words, such as *thesaurus* (a soft *th* sound, as in *thistle*, and the emphasis on the second syllable), using the phonetic symbols explained at the front of the dictionary
- Checking whether a word usually has a capital

Thesauruses

Recommendations

- *The Penguin Thesaurus*, by Rosalind Fergusson, Martin Manser and David Pickering, 2004

A thesaurus has two main uses: finding a word that's on the tip of your tongue, and getting a synonym for an overused word. If, for example, you know there's a medical word meaning 'prediction of how an illness will go' but you just can't think what it is, you could look it up in the thesaurus. Look up 'predict' in the index at the back, and it tells you where to find words connected to prediction. Leaf through to that page and the second word is 'prognosis'.

However, it isn't always that easy to know where to look, and the words listed can be very disparate – especially in Roget's Thesaurus, the original thesaurus, first printed in 1852 and still the most popular. Make sure you use the dictionary to check any word you find. For example, looking for another word for *boat* in Roget gives me 'wherry', 'steam-packet', 'armada' and 'seventy-four', among many others – not terms that can be used interchangeably. *The Penguin Thesaurus* is much better organized than Roget, but you will still need to check words in a dictionary.

Uses
- Finding words that are on the tip of your tongue
- Getting alternatives for overused words
- Expanding your vocabulary
- Helping to solve crosswords

Style guides

Recommendations

- *The Economist Style Guide*, by *The Economist*, 2003

Every newspaper and magazine has its own style guide which its journalists and editors use to find out the publication's 'house style'. When it comes to spelling, capitalization and so on, there are often several forms that are equally correct or well-used, such as single quotes (') or double quotes ("). But publications want to be consistent, so as to avoid confusing their readers – you don't want to be reading about Col. Gadafy (the *Guardian*) on one page and Colonel Gaddafi (*The Times*) on the next. Style guides set out each publication's line on these things, as well as laying down its approach to hyphens, split infinitives and other tricky areas.

Style guides reflect the personalities of the publications. The *Guardian*'s is very modern, especially in terms of capitals and punctuation, whereas *The Times*'s is very conservative – a lot of its online style guide is taken up with the correct forms for royal, military and aristocratic titles. It tells you, for instance, that 'no wife of a baronet or knight takes her Christian name in her title unless she is the daughter of a duke, a marquess or an earl.' Both publications currently have versions of their style guides on their websites.

For most people, especially in business, *The Economist* gets the right balance between modern and conservative. At the time of writing, you can use a free, cut-down version of its style guide on its website, but its printed style guide is easier to refer to. And, among many other useful touches, it includes a full list of editor's marks.

The book you're reading now also deals with a lot of the material you'd find in a style guide – mostly in the rest of this section.

Uses

- Bringing consistency to spelling, capitalization and punctuation
- Covering some of the points you'd find in a usage guide

Usage guides

Recommendations

- *The New Fowler's Modern English Usage*, Third Edition, by R. W. Burchfield, 2004

Usage guides tell you the best way to use specific words and phrases, dealing with common mistakes and linguistic controversies. A good usage guide should be able to tell you how to use the word *respectively* without embarrassing yourself, or how to hyphenate properly – as will this book. However, usage guides go further, giving advice on the use of rarer terms such as *ergo* and *betwixt*. They can be a little too abstruse for some readers, as in this passage from Fowler on glasses:

In AmE *eyeglasses* is commonly used instead of the simplex *glasses*, but, though the *OED* gives 19c. examples of *eyeglasses* in BrE use, this longer term is hardly ever encountered now in the UK.

However, after a dictionary and a style guide, a usage guide is one of the most useful books you can have. The remaining chapters of this book deal with the most common usage problems, but if you want more, I suggest *Fowler's Modern English Usage*. To be consistent, it is best to settle on one usage guide and stick to it.

I recommend the third edition of Fowler because it is modern and widely used. But in many ways I prefer the tone of the first and second editions, which were written by Fowler himself in the twenties. Before these books, he wrote *The King's English*, published in 1908, and this is still well worth reading. At the time of writing, this can be read or downloaded from a very useful site called Bartleby.com, an online collection of books which are no longer under copyright. Another useful book, *The Elements of Style*, by William Strunk, is also available.

Uses
- Settling arguments with colleagues about what is right
- Resolving uncertainties
- Browsing through for advice

Grammar guides

Recommendations

- *Making Sense of Grammar*, by David Crystal, 2004

If you get interested in grammar and want to read about it in greater depth, I recommend *Rediscover Grammar* or *Making Sense of Grammar* by David Crystal. David

Crystal is probably the greatest all-round expert on the English language, and he has a very useful and pragmatic approach to grammar which enables him to avoid the dry pedantry the subject can encourage. It's worth remembering that the way experts approach grammar has changed a great deal since the fifties and sixties. Until then, grammar was based on rigid categories and rules derived from the way Latin works. Since then, it has become much more fluid, and more interested in describing how language is really used.

For anyone who is really fascinated by English, its grammar, history and the way it is used, I'd recommend the hefty *Cambridge Encyclopedia of the English Language*, also by David Crystal.

Other tools

Finally, two very useful – and free – editing tools that are often overlooked: your voice, and the editing symbols you use.

Your voice
Perhaps the most neglected of the tools at your disposal is your voice. It is immensely useful for:

• Checking your tone
• Making sure you're not tripping your readers up
• Punctuating
• Making sure your sentences work

Because writing gives no overt information about pitch or expression, there are plenty of things that work in conversation that don't work on the page. There is, for example, no sympathy mark or contrition mark to go with the exclamation mark; there is no punctuation mark or accent that says the equivalent of 'trying not to laugh'. In a spoken conversation this can make the difference between a joke and a terrible insult. We all know people who lard their writing with exclamation marks in an attempt to replicate on the page what they may do very well with their voice. But the exclamation mark, especially in bulk, is too blunt an instrument; it cannot communicate the difference between 'Get out!!!' bellowed in anger, and 'Get out!!!' as a camp expression of mock disbelief.

The only way to test whether writing will really work for your reader on the page is to read it out and see how much work your voice has to do. If it works in calm, well-modulated tones (I'm thinking of David Attenborough narrating a wildlife documentary) then it will probably work on the page. If not, you probably need to think again. I recently did some one-to-one coaching with a man who wrote letters for his company, and showed him, by reading out a sentence, how his writing made the reader do too much work. It was perfectly grammatical, but just too difficult to read. And its difficulty was reflected in the amount of work my voice had to do in order to make sense of its many sub-clauses.

If you can read something out to yourself without tripping over your words or having to carry the meaning with your voice, then your reader should understand it as you intend. As you read it out, noticing where you pause will help you to punctuate it. For example, the word I most often see causing punctuation problems is *however*. People seem to see it as having its own built-in punctuation, which frees them from the need to use full-stops or commas with it. This is a typical example:

This was entirely due to human error however it has caused you a great deal of distress.

But if you read this out, you'll find that you have to make a full-stop's worth of pause before it and a comma's worth after it for it to make sense:

This was entirely due to human error. However, it has caused you a great deal of distress.

Putting punctuation where you pause solves many common problems.

Editing marks

Most of the time, the marks you make when editing your own work are just for you, but even so, you need to have some consistency so that you can remember what you meant by a particular symbol. Professional proofreaders, whose marks are used by printers and page-setters they may never meet, have lots of very specific marks, because what they mean must be absolutely unambiguous. For my own purposes, I find that the following are enough:

Function	Mark
Paragraph break	This book is for anyone who has to write at work. ¶ It is for all of you who write most days, but have never been told how.

Function	Mark
Italics	This book is for <u>anyone</u> who has to write at work. It is for all of you who write most days, but have never been told how.
Bold *bold*	This book is for anyone who has to <u>write</u> at work. It is for all of you who write most days, but have never been told how.
Capitals	This book is for anyone who has to write at work. <u>it</u> is for all of you who write most days, but have never been told how.
Lower case	This book is for anyone who has to write at ⌐Work. It is for all of you who write most days, but have never been told how.
Insert	This book is for anyone who has to write ᵃᵗ work. It is for all of you who write most ∧ days, but have never been told how.
Delete	This book is for anyone who has to write |often| at work. It is for all of you who write most days, but have never been told how.
Punctuation	This book is for anyone who has to write at wo⌐rk. It⌐ is for all of you who write most days, but have never been told how.

13
Punctuation

The main point of punctuation is to guide your reader's understanding. If you can show by punctuation how to read your writing aloud, then you have succeeded. The other function of punctuation is to show that you know the rules. People are much more likely to respect your writing if you get the details and technicalities right. To do this, you have to know how the various punctuation marks work.

Apostrophes '

Apostrophes are the most frequently misused pieces of punctuation, yet they are very easy to get right. If you want an easy, quick way of making yourself seem a better writer, they are a good place to start.

Only use an apostrophe for two things:

1. To show that letters are missing from the word (cont'd = continued), especially in contractions – when two separate words have been turned into one: don't = do not.

2. To show the possessive: *Jim's pen* = the pen that belongs to Jim; *two weeks' notice* = the notice of two weeks.

If you know the situations in which people tend to go wrong, you can learn the right rule. Here are the main accident black spots:

Abbreviations
Don't use an apostrophe for the plural of an abbreviation: *the MPs are voting* (not *the MP's are voting*), *there was a conference of CIOs, we need five new PCs.*

Decades
Refer to the eighties as the 1980s or '80s, not the 1980's.

Its and it's
Don't use an apostrophe for possessive pronouns like *his, hers, yours, theirs* and *its.* If you mean 'it is', use *it's.* If you mean 'belonging to it', use *its. It's a good dog that knows its master.*

Whose and who's
Use an apostrophe if you really mean 'who is', as in: *Who's this then?* Otherwise (to talk about possession) use *whose: Whose shoes are these?* Here are both in the same sentence: *Who's the man whose shoes are in the hall?*

Plurals ending in s

If a plural ends in *s*, like *customers*, then show something belongs to it by just adding an apostrophe to the end: *All our customers' orders are sent to head office.*

Singulars ending in s

If a singular noun ends in *s*, then add apostrophe *s* as usual, unless you wouldn't pronounce the *s*: I would say *Achilles' heel*, but *Chris's pen*.

To be absolutely sure of whether your apostrophe is right, answer the question on page 195:

Brackets ( )

Brackets provide extra information, but they tend to break the rhythm and flow of the sentence. Try to avoid them if you can, except to give dry or technical information that is somehow outside the rest of the piece of writing:

- Where to look

  Sales have almost doubled over the past five years (see chart below).

- Equivalent measures

  A £240m ($430m) lawsuit against the newspaper has been launched.

- References

  The news on pension reform (*The Times*, 'Pensions to be reformed', 4 September 2004) . . .

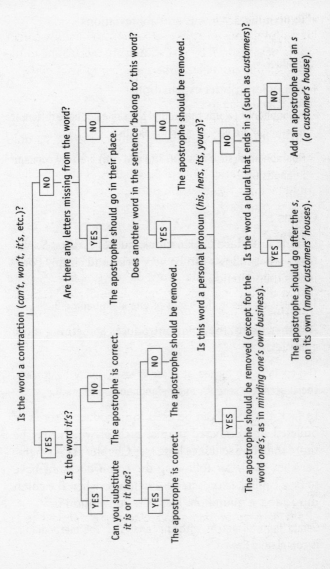

Is the word a contraction (*can't, won't, it's,* etc.)?

YES — Is the word *it's*?

YES — Can you substitute *it is* or *it has*?

YES — The apostrophe is correct.

NO — The apostrophe should be removed.

NO — The apostrophe is correct.

NO — Are there any letters missing from the word?

YES — The apostrophe should go in their place.

NO — Does another word in the sentence 'belong to' this word?

YES — Is this word a personal pronoun (*his, hers, its, yours*)?

YES — The apostrophe should be removed (except for the word *one's*, as in *minding one's own business*).

NO — Is the word a plural that ends in *s* (such as *customers*)?

YES — The apostrophe should go after the *s*, on its own (*many customers' houses*).

NO — Add an apostrophe and an *s* (*a customer's house*).

NO — The apostrophe should be removed.

- Explaining acronyms and abbreviations

  The FSA (Food Standards Agency) has approved our new product.

- Examples or brief explanations

  Homophones (words that sound the same but have different meanings) are very common in English.

  Homophones (such as *sight*, *site* and *cite*) are very common in English.

Colons :

Colons introduce explanations, quotes or lists. Sometimes what follows can be very brief and simply completes the sentence:

The decision was in the hands of one man: George Bush.

At other times, the colon introduces something more complex:

The commission looked at these areas: primary healthcare, social services, schools, and neighbourhood renewal.

In fact, the colon can be used to introduce a series of bulleted or numbered points, each of which may be more than one sentence long (see Chapter 11). Remember that the letter following the colon does not have to be a capital, except in US English or when the colon introduces a quotation. Here the convention is:

Gerald Dunn disagrees with this analysis: 'The methodology is completely flawed.'

Commas ,

A comma tells the reader to take a short pause in order to make the different parts of a sentence clearer. Commas are very versatile pieces of punctuation, but they have two main functions.

Separating a comment from the rest of the sentence
Fifty years ago, according to the mayor, the town was full of holidaymakers from the cities.

In this example, *according to the mayor* interrupts the rest of the sentence in order to give you a bit of extra information. Here the commas are working rather like brackets, but without breaking the rhythm of the sentence. Commas are often used in this way to give a description of someone:

Junichiro Koizumi, the Japanese prime minister, will introduce sweeping changes to the financial system.

Always remember the second in these pairs of commas. People very often forget it, which can make sentences more difficult to understand.

It must always be possible to remove a comment like this without messing the sentence up. In the examples above, you could remove the comment and the sentence would still make sense – even though it might not supply all the information the reader needs. This is a common type of mistake:

We re-examined the figures, and much to our surprise, found that there was a mistake.

Here, it is impossible to remove *and much to our surprise* without damaging the sentence. The first comma is on the wrong side of the *and*. The sentence should read:

We re-examined the figures and, much to our surprise, found that there was a mistake.

Much to our surprise can be removed without damaging the sentence.

Separating items in lists
The commission looked at these areas: primary healthcare, social services, schools, and neighbourhood renewal.

In this example, each item is separated from the others by a comma. Without the final comma, it would be easy to read the last two items as one: schools and neighbourhood renewal, or the renewal of schools and the neighbourhood. It's perfectly acceptable to use a comma before *and* in order to prevent misunderstandings like this.

This also applies to descriptions, but only if you could replace the comma with the word *and*. *This profitable, successful company is making history* is right, and *this profitable limited company is making history* is also right, because *limited company* is a single item. It is not a company that is limited, but a very specific type of company – a limited liability company – that is usually referred to as a limited company for short. You could not refer to *this profitable and limited company*, so you should not put a comma between the words.

Don't use a comma to join two complete sentences

Never use a comma to join two complete sentences, as in the following (incorrect) example:

If you arrive on Wednesday I won't be there, come on Thursday instead.

A complete sentence has a verb in it, and makes sense on its own. There are two sentences in the example above:

If you arrive on Wednesday I won't be there. Come on Thursday instead.

If you want to use a comma, you need a connecting word like *so* or *but*:

If you arrive on Wednesday I won't be there, so come on Thursday instead.

Alternatively, you can use a semicolon:

If you arrive on Wednesday I won't be there; come on Thursday instead.

There's more on semicolons later in this chapter.

Dashes –

Dashes look a bit like hyphens, but they're wider – usually about the width of a letter 'n'. Microsoft Word turns hyphens into dashes if it thinks it's appropriate, but it can miss some. To insert a dash manually, hold down Ctrl and press the Minus key on your numeric keypad.

Dashes are very dynamic – they keep writing moving

along quickly and they add a hint of drama. Some people never use dashes, because they can be more or less replaced by other pieces of punctuation – mainly commas, colons and brackets.

Dashes working like commas

Fifty years ago – according to the mayor – the town was full of holidaymakers from the cities.

Here a comment is separated from the rest of the sentence by a pair of dashes, rather than a pair of commas. Using dashes seems to speed the sentence up, and adds emphasis to the comment. The effect of this depends on the context – here it could make it sound as though the mayor's opinions were being doubted.

Dashes working like colons

The decision was in the hands of one man – George Bush.

Changing this colon to a dash makes the sentence seem somehow less grave and more urgent.

Dashes working like brackets

The works of three great authors – Anthony Trollope, George Eliot and Charles Dickens – have recently been adapted for TV.

This example shows how dashes are very useful for giving examples or essential details. Brackets here would have made the names seem less important; commas would have been confusing because of the commas separating the names. Dashes keep the sentence moving, make it clear – and imply that the names are essential information.

Dashes representing ranges
Dashes can also show ranges: *x–y* means 'from x to y'
or 'between x and y':

Turnover is growing by 5–10 per cent a year.

Or:

We have 3,000–6,000 different products in stock at any time.

In general, it is better to spell ranges out in words.
Never use a mixture of phrase and dash. Say *He was
40–45 years old* or *He was between 40 and 45 years
old*, but not *He was between 40–45 years old*. Some
publications, such as *The Economist*, use hyphens to
show ranges. You can use either a hyphen or a dash,
as long as you use them consistently.

Exclamation marks !

An exclamation mark marks an exclamation, such as:
Hello! or *Oh!* Using them in any other way is a bad
idea – especially using them to show that you really
mean something, or that you intend something to be
funny. People who start to do this tend to use more and
more exclamation marks in a bid to make their writing
look more and more surprising and funny, with the
opposite effect. If something doesn't work without an
exclamation mark, then it won't work with one.

Full stops .

No one misuses full stops: they end a sentence. But people do miss full stops out sometimes, using either a comma or the word 'and' instead. Here's an example:

Thank you for your letter and I am extremely pleased to hear that your problems have been resolved.

If you can replace an *and* with a full stop then do. It will make your sentences shorter and easier to understand. In this example, the writer has thanked the customer for their letter. He then moves on to a separate point about being pleased to hear something. The two points do not need to be connected by the word *and*, so it should be replaced by a full stop.

The word that most frequently causes people to miss out full stops is *however*:

Believing that you had £120 in your account, you tried to withdraw £40 however an earlier payment into your account had not cleared.

Here, the sentence should end after '£40'. The writer has told us about an action – trying to withdraw £40 – and the belief that inspired the action. The word *however* begins a new point, a new idea that is different to the one we have just been told. A new point requires a new sentence:

Believing that you had £120 in your account, you tried to withdraw £40. However, an earlier payment into your account had not cleared.

Abbreviations

Full stops are also used to mark abbreviations (such as *etc.*) when they don't end with the same letter as the full word. You would write *Prof. Smith* (for a professor), but *Dr Jones* (for a doctor). It used to be standard practice to put full stops after each letter in an initialism, such as *N.A.T.O.*, but we don't do this nowadays because there are so many of them – it would break the writing up too much.

Hyphens -

Hyphens are used to show that words have been linked together to form a new term. They are mostly used to show that two or more words are being used as a single adjective:

What will happen in the long term? The long-term view is good.

Does this mortgage have a fixed rate? This is a fixed-rate mortgage.

How do we use it from day to day? Its day-to-day use is as a catalyst.

In each of the examples above, the first sentence doesn't require hyphens: *term* is a noun, modified by the single adjective *long*. However, the second sentence does require hyphens: *view* is a noun modified by the compound adjective *long-term*.

Hyphens are also used in:

- Fractions: two-thirds, three-quarters
- Preventing misunderstanding: presenting something

again is *re-presenting*, with the hyphen distinguishing it from the word *representing*.

Question marks ?

If a sentence is a question, then it should end in a question mark. The only mistake people sometimes make is to use question marks in sentences like this:

I asked him whether I could have a day's leave?

The sentence above is a statement, so it doesn't need a question mark, even though it is talking about a question.

The other situation that sometimes causes confusion is when an instruction is given in question form:

Could you let me have your final decision by the end of the day?

Although I believe this needs a question mark, it is becoming increasingly common for good writers to leave the question mark out. This is presumably because they want the recipient to do as they're told, but they don't want to appear rude. This seems wrong to me: if you don't want something to sound like a question, just use the word please:

Please let me have your final decision by the end of the day.

Quotation marks " or '

There are two kinds of quotation mark: single (') and double (") inverted commas. In the UK, newspapers and magazines tend to use double inverted commas (also called 'double quotes') whereas books tend to use single ones. Which you choose is your own preference, but you must be consistent. And whichever you choose, use the other style for quotes within quotes:

Mr Mulvery added: 'What that newspaper calls "gross inefficiency" is actually good sense.'

There are three ways of using quotation marks:

- For marking out direct speech – giving the actual words a person spoke

  The prime minister said, 'The future is bright.'

- For the titles of articles, songs and poems (titles of books, films, plays and newspapers are usually italicized rather than put in quotes, e.g. *The Economist*)

  He was singing 'Waterloo Sunset' again.

- To show that a word or phrase is being used in an unusual, ironic or technical way

  These 'taxes' were nothing of the sort: they were blackmail.

Be very careful with this last use – only use quotation marks here if it would be confusing not to have them, and don't use them just to add emphasis.

Punctuation in direct quotes

When writing direct speech, the first quotation mark can come at the beginning of the sentence:

'When I was a boy', said Mr Williams . . .

Or after a comma:

Mr Williams said, 'When I was a boy . . .'

This is used with words like *said*, *added* and *commented* when they are introducing speech.

The first quotation mark can also follow a colon:

Mr Williams disagreed: 'When I was a boy . . .'

This is used when the quote illustrates or explains the statement before the colon.

You can also use direct quotations as part of a sentence, with no punctuation apart from the quotation marks:

According to Thomas Hobbes, life in a state of nature is 'nasty, brutish and short', but . . .

Use this style of quotation to weave someone else's words into the point you are making.

Many people have difficulty knowing where to put the punctuation when using quotation marks: does it go inside or outside? The answer is easy: if the punctuation is part of the quote then it goes inside the marks, if it is not part of the quote then it goes outside the marks.

In the following example the comma shows a pause in the person's speech and the full stop shows the end of their speech, so the punctuation goes inside the quotation marks:

'I can't say for sure,' he said, 'at least until I've seen more evidence.'

Whereas in the next example the punctuation does not belong to the speech, but to the sentence around it, so it goes outside the quotation marks:

'I'm not sure', he said, 'whether that's true', and he went on to make a very long-winded point about 'the requirement for fiscal rectitude'.

Semicolons ;

Semicolons have two uses: they separate complex items in a list, and they stick together two sentences that are very closely related. People most often use semicolons for the first purpose:

The conference will be attended by the following people: Mr Pell, vice-president of AcmeCo; Mrs Barabas, chief executive of International Halva; and Graham Bison, financial director of MortriCare.

Semicolons are necessary in this list in order to make it clear that the titles belong to the names. Without semicolons working as 'super commas', there is no unambiguous way to give this list. Only use semicolons in this way if it is confusing to use commas.

The second role of semicolons, sticking together two sentences that depend upon one another, is mostly only exercised by people to show that they know how to do it; it is almost never essential to use semicolons in this way.

Spaces

Use spaces in the same way that publishers do:

- Full stops, colons, semicolons, question marks and exclamation marks never have a space before them and always have one after them.
- Commas follow the same rule, except in numbers, e.g. 2,500 or 3,314,217.
- Sentences have only one space in between them, not two.
- Quotation marks always sit right next to the word they enclose.
- Apostrophes don't have any effect on spacing.

You can see these rules being broken in the following example. For clarity's sake, spaces are indicated by dots:

'·Good·Lord·!··Have·you·really·won·£·2·,·500·,· 000·on·the·lottery·?·'··he·asked·,·incredulously··.

Instead, write the sentence like this:

'Good Lord! Have you really won £2,500,000 on the lottery?' he asked, incredulously.

If you think it looks too cramped, change the font or the character spacing in your word processor.

14
Rules and Conventions

The more your writing looks like the kind of writing people are used to reading in books, newspapers and magazines, the more authoritative you will seem. You can achieve this by learning a relatively small number of rules and conventions.

&

Never use the ampersand sign except in the name of a company: *Marks & Spencer* is fine, but *Our CEO & marketing director* is not.

Capitals

Capital letters can be tricky, because they are governed by a peculiar mixture of very clear rules and very hazy conventions. First the clear rules.

Always capitalize:

1. The first letter of a sentence

2. The personal pronoun *I*

3. The names of people (Gordon Brown)

4. Companies (General Electric)

5. Trade names (the Remington Fuzz-Away)

6. Specific places (Manchester, France)

7. Adjectives relating to places (Mancunian buildings, French foreign policy)

8. The inhabitants of places (some Mancunians, the French)

9. Languages (Latin, Mandarin)

10. Days of the week and months of the year (Tuesday, September) – but not the seasons (spring, autumn)

11. Recognized historical periods (the Middle Ages, the Enlightenment)

12. Public holidays (Boxing Day, Remembrance Sunday)

13. Religions and important religious terms (Catholicism, Purim, Mass)

14. Titles of books, plays, works of art, articles, etc. (*The Mill on the Floss*, Rodin's *The Thinker*) – but not the small connecting words within them (*the, a, of, in, upon*), unless one is the first word

15. Newspapers and other publications (only *The Economist* and *The Times* have capital *T*s for *The*) – these names are usually italicized

Now for the hazy conventions. These cover two areas:

- People's titles (Her Majesty the Queen, but the queens of England)
- Unique things (the moon, the equator, the Internet)

The basic rule for titles is:

Use capitals when the title is unique or important and lower case when the title is descriptive or generic.

Different publications and authorities have different interpretations of this. *Black Rod* and the *First Lord of the Treasury* should obviously be capitalized, but what about terms like *the prime minister* and *the government*? Well, if you're speaking about them in general terms they should definitely be lower case: *no government can guarantee full employment, five prime ministers met in Lisbon on Sunday*. If you are speaking of a specific government or prime minister, you have the option of capitalizing, but you must be consistent.

The Economist never capitalizes these terms, but many other publications do. I favour *The Economist*'s rule, because it reduces the number of distracting capitals on the page. This is especially useful at work, where people's official titles tend to be descriptive and generic, such as *chairman, chief executive officer, sales assistant, regional manager*. A whole page of such titles in capitals makes a document look baffling, especially when there are also lots of capitalized product names. Keeping all the titles lower case simplifies things a lot. Of course, when you sign your name you would give your job-title capitals, but not in other situations.

There are some unique things, such as the moon or

the equator, which you might expect to have capitals, but which don't. There are also things, such as the Internet, that don't really name a specific thing, but do usually have capitals. In these cases, the moon and the equator are taken to be descriptions, and the Internet has come to be thought of as a specific thing. If you're not sure whether the convention is to capitalize something like this, look in a dictionary: if the word is capitalized there, you should capitalize it in your writing.

The most common mistakes with capitalizing are:

- Capitalizing every noun or important phrase
- Capitalizing any word that could refer to a specific person. Some people prefer to capitalize terms like *the Prime Minister*, because that is a title, but there is no excuse for capitalizing descriptive terms like *your daughter*, or *our sales assistants*, because they are generic or descriptive terms.

I and me

Which you use depends on whether the word is the subject or the object. The subject is the person or thing that takes action (*I greeted him*) while the object is the person or thing that is acted upon (*He greeted me*). People only really get this wrong in three ways:

When there are two subjects
Me and John went to Manchester. *(wrong)*

In this case, you just have to remove the other name to see that this is wrong: you would never say *Me went to Manchester*. Both you and John are the subjects of the sentence, so it should read:

John and I went to Manchester.

When there are two objects

Sarah had lunch with John and I. *(wrong)*

Again, you just have to remove the other name to see that the sentence is wrong. It should read:

Sarah had lunch with John and me.

After a preposition

This is between you and I. *or* Between you and I, . . . *(wrong)*

A preposition is a small word (such as *about, of, by, at, in, to, with, under, above, on, into, before, since, between* and *up*) which indicates how some other word affects a noun. Some examples of how they affect the meaning of a noun are:

- They talked to me.
- They talked about me.
- They talked without me.

Any noun that has been affected by a preposition becomes the object of its own clause, even if it's right at the beginning of a sentence. That's why you say *To me it seems obvious* instead of *To I it seems obvious*. It is also why the sentence above should be:

This is between you and me *or* Between you and me, . . .

Numbers

In general, you should spell out the numbers one to nine, and then use figures for the number 10 onwards. However, you should never begin a sentence with a figure, because it looks messy. At the beginning of a sentence, you should spell the number out, or rework the sentence to avoid it.

Not: 23 members of staff transferred . . .
But: Twenty-three members of staff transferred . . .
Or: Out of a staff of 136, 23 members transferred . . .

If you are giving lots of numbers, and comparing them, it is best to use figures for all of them: *In 1995, we had 124 staff in 5 offices with 30 vans.* But you should still not begin a sentence with a figure.

That and which (and the comma)

Microsoft's Grammar Check says that *which* should always have a comma in front of it. This isn't true. In fact, there are two ways of using *which*:

With a comma
Send all the letters, which are signed.

This sentence tells you to send all the letters, and it gives a bit of extra information – they're signed. With a comma, *which* is an addition – the object here is *all the letters. Which* here describes the letters to be sent.

Without a comma
Send all the letters which are signed.

This sentence implies that some letters are signed and some are unsigned. You should send only the signed letters. Without a comma, *which* is an inextricable part of the word to which it is attached – the object here is *all the letters which are signed*. *Which* here defines the letters to be sent.

The word *that* can only be used without a comma. It can define, but not describe. In fact, in sentences like the second one, it is best to use *that*:

Send all the letters that are signed.

They and he/she

Until fairly recently, most writers used the pronoun *he* when referring to someone whose gender they didn't know. It would be common to say, for example: *Tell your reader what he needs to know*. More and more people find this sexist, along with other 'gendered language', such as referring to *mankind* rather than *humankind* or *the chairman* rather than *the chairperson* or simply *the chair*.

There are three alternatives, each with advantages and disadvantages. I recommend them in this order:

Rewrite the sentence
It is usually possible to rewrite the sentence to avoid the problem. The easiest way of doing this is to make the noun plural. Instead of the example above, we could write: *Tell your readers what they need to know*.

Use he *and* she *an equal number of times*

Sometimes it is impossible to make the noun plural, especially when giving examples and instructions. It would be difficult to make this sentence plural: *If the passenger still refuses to show you his passport, do not admit him.* In a longer piece of writing, you can get around this by alternating between *she* and *he* for your examples (but not within a single example). Thus, the example above would be fine, as long as there was another example with the feminine pronoun: *When the first passenger arrives, show her to her seat.* That is mostly what I have done in this book.

Use they

People have used *they* to mean 'he or she' for a long time, but it has always been looked down upon in formal writing. It is becoming more acceptable now, especially in emails and other writing with an informal or personal tone. I predict that this will be normal even in formal writing within five or ten years, but it isn't yet – which is why I recommend you try the alternatives above first.

Use he or she

This is correct, but too clumsy to be used repeatedly because it produces sentences like this: *If a customer is lost, ask him or her where he or she wants to go.*

To boldly split infinitives

The most famous split infinitive is in the voiceover at the beginning of *Star Trek*:

These are the voyages of the Starship Enterprise. Its five-year mission: to boldly go where no man has gone before.

Here, the infinitive verb *to go* is split by the adverb *boldly*.

The prejudice against splitting infinitives grew up in the nineteenth century, when grammarians were trying to lay down rules for English grammar based on those of Latin. Because the infinitives of Latin verbs are single words, such as *vadere*, they cannot be split. Therefore, the grammarians argued, English infinitives should be treated as a single unit, even though they consist of two words: *to go*, *to run*, *to speak*, etc.

The reasoning for this 'rule' is absurd, but there is an advantage in observing it in business writing: your readers might think less of you if you don't. Many people loathe split infinitives, and harshly judge those who use them – despite the fact that pretty much all the great English writers have split infinitives whenever they felt like it.

It is usually easy enough to move the adverb and, in general, it is best to put it after the infinitive:

to boldly go = to go boldly (better than *boldly to go*)

Or you can move it to the end of the clause:

In order to quickly overtake our competitors, we will need to massively increase our advertising budget.

This could become:

In order to overtake our competitors quickly, we will need to increase our advertising budget massively.

However, if avoiding splitting the infinitive makes the sentence ambiguous or confusing, as in the following example, then you should split it.

The oil companies are expected to refuse immediately to reduce prices.

The example above could mean that the oil companies are going to reject any kind of reduction. But it could equally mean that they will reject only an immediate reduction – perhaps implying that they have agreed to a longer-term reduction. To resolve it, we must split an infinitive:

The oil companies are expected to refuse to immediately reduce prices.

Or, better still, rewrite it:

Experts do not expect the oil companies to reduce prices immediately.

Who and whom

Many people use *whom* as though it were the posh version of *who*, to be used when you want to inject a touch of class into a sentence. It isn't, and if you are at all unsure about the rules, it is best just to use *who* every time. *Whom* now sounds rather formal, and even very good writers often prefer the more conversational *who*.

Use whom *after a preposition – usually*

This is quite an easy rule to apply, and, despite what I said above, it still sounds odd not to do it:

To who did you send the letter?

Who did you send the letter to?

These examples are both wrong, although the second one is what most people would say in conversation. Because *to* is a preposition, this is the correct way of writing the sentence:

To whom did you address the letter?

Other correct examples are:

For whom is it intended?
By whom was it sent?
With whom did you arrive?
In whom should I confide?

To find out whether a word is a preposition, look it up in the dictionary. If the word says *prep.* beside it, it is a preposition.

The preposition rule is a part of the main rule below, which is easy to state but needs a bit of interpretation.

Use whom *when it is the object of its own clause*

Both of these sentences are correct:

I like the man who helped us yesterday.

I like the man whom we helped yesterday.

A clause is a part of a sentence that works a bit like a mini-sentence. The subject of a clause is the person or thing who is taking action, and the object of the clause is the person or thing who is being acted upon.

In the first sentence, *who* is part of the clause *who helped us yesterday*. If we rewrite it as a separate sentence, we get: *The man helped us yesterday.* In this clause, *the man* is the subject, because he is the one doing the helping. That is why we use *who*, because it is functioning as the subject of its clause.

In the second sentence, *whom* is part of the clause *whom we helped yesterday*. If we rewrite this as a separate sentence, we get: *We helped the man yesterday.* In this clause, *the man* is the object, because he is the one being helped. That is why we use *whom*, because it is functioning as the object of its clause.

Here are two more correct examples:

We gave the job to someone who has plenty of energy.

As a sentence, the clause is *Someone has plenty of energy.* *Who* is taking the place of the subject.

Our CEO, whom everyone respects, has resigned.

As a sentence, the clause is *Everyone respects our CEO.* *Whom* is taking the place of the object.

This example is also correct, even though *who* comes after a preposition:

There is some confusion about who should go.

As a sentence, the clause is *[Someone] should go.* *Who* is taking the place of the subject.

This works because the clause rule takes precedence over the preposition rule.

Beginning and ending sentences

I have found that a lot of people have hang-ups or misgivings about words that begin or end sentences. Often, they have made up their own rules, such as 'never begin a sentence with "because"' or 'never end a sentence with a two-letter word'. The real rule is:

Begin or end sentences with whatever words you like.

The reason for the worry is that some authorities dislike sentences that begin with the words *and* or *but*, and dislike sentences that end with a preposition. Sentences like this can sound clumsy or inelegant, but there is nothing grammatically wrong with them. *And* or *but* can be strong, oratorical ways of starting a sentence. But if you do it too often, it can become irritating. And a preposition isn't always the most elegant word to end a sentence with. But people can tie themselves up in knots trying to find an alternative with which to end. One of Winston Churchill's speechwriters had a particular aversion to ending sentences with prepositions, and was prepared to mangle his writing in spectacular ways to avoid it, until Churchill told him: 'This is the kind of language up with which I will not put.'

15
Words to Watch

Misspelling

Most people use computers with spellchecking software to write at work, so straightforward misspellings of words like *necessary* are becoming rarer and rarer. The danger these days comes when you misspell a word in such a way that it becomes the correct spelling of another word. This can happen because of a slip of the typist's finger, so that *your* becomes *you*, or it can happen because you don't know the different spellings of words that sound the same, such as *site* and *cite*. The first means 'to put something (especially a building) in a particular place', while the second means 'to invoke an authority or other evidence to support a proposition'.

The following list contains the words that people most frequently misspell at work – usually because they have confused two words that sound the same or similar, but have very different meanings.

adverse/averse
Adverse means 'bad', as in *adverse weather conditions*. *Averse* means that you don't like something, as in *I'm not averse to the odd drink*, meaning 'I like drinking'.

advice/advise
Advice is the noun and *advise* is the verb, as with *licence* and *license*. When I advise you, I give you advice.

affect/effect
Usually, when you affect something, you have an effect on it. So *affect* is a verb and *effect* is a noun. The only exception is that *affect* can mean 'emotion' and *effect* can mean 'to make or to put into effect'. In general though, just remember that when you affect something you have an effect on it.

allude
To allude to something is to refer to it without mentioning it explicitly. If you talked about *the gentleman at number ten* you might be alluding to the prime minister.

alternate/alternative
People often use *alternate* when they should say *alternative*. *Alternate* cannot be used to mean 'different', as in *alternate reality*. It should be *alternative reality*. *Alternately* means 'by turns'; *alternatively*, meaning 'instead', is usually what the writer meant to say.

appraise/apprise

To appraise something is to estimate its quality or value. To apprise someone of something is to tell them about it. It is better not to use *apprise* in any case, since *tell* is always a more direct and useful way of saying the same thing.

aural/oral

Aural has to do with the ears, whereas *oral* has to do with the mouth. They are both pronounced the same way.

bought/brought

Many people don't make a distinction between these two words in speech, but it's important to be clear about them in writing. *Bought* is the past tense of *to buy*; *brought* is the past tense of *to bring*.

chose/choose

Chose (rhyming with hose) is the past tense; *choose* (rhyming with shoes) is the present tense. People often get these mixed up – perhaps because of *lose* (rhyming with shoes) and *loose* (rhyming with moose), which operate on a different principle.

compare to/compare with

Use *to* when comparing two very different types of thing, as in the metaphorical phrase *Shall I compare thee to a summer's day?* Use *with* when the things are very alike, as in the concrete *Earnings this year were low compared with last year's.*

compliment/complement
A compliment is a nice thing to say about someone, whereas a complement is a full set. A pair of shoes complements someone's outfit if they complete it. Things you get without paying are complimentary, as they're given to you as a compliment, rather than to make up a set.

comprise
Comprise means 'contain': the whole comprises the parts. So *a three-piece suit comprises jacket, trousers and waistcoat* is right, but *jacket, trousers and waistcoat comprise a three-piece suit* and *a three-piece suit is comprised of jacket, trousers and waistcoat* are wrong.

continual/continuous
Continual means 'frequently', whereas *continuous* means 'constantly'. A continuous process is one that is uninterrupted. Continual improvements are ones that are made often, but not necessarily 24 hours a day. *Continuous* doesn't have to relate to time: an unbroken line is continuous.

councillor/counsellor
A councillor is a member of a council, whereas a counsellor is someone who provides counsel (advice).

defuse/diffuse
You defuse a bomb or a tense situation. *Diffuse* means 'scattered'.

discreet/discrete
Something *discreet* is hidden, or at least not drawn attention to, whereas something *discrete* is separate. I remember this by thinking that Crete is separate from the rest of Greece, but not hidden.

disinterested/uninterested
Disinterested means 'impartial or unbiased', whereas *uninterested* means 'bored'. It's good to have a disinterested judge, but not an uninterested one.

draw/drawer
Remember that the sliding compartment of your desk where you keep pens, paperclips and doughnuts is a drawer, not a draw. *Top drawer*, meaning 'excellent', comes from the place where people keep their jewels.

e.g./i.e.
E.g. stands for the Latin phrase 'exempli gratia' and means 'for example'. *I.e.* stands for 'id est' and means 'that is to say'. In proper, flowing text, write *for example* or *that is to say*, keeping *e.g.* and *i.e.* for brackets, notes and footnotes.

ensure/insure/assure
Ensure means 'to make sure' (usually that something happens). *Insure* means 'to take out insurance'. *Assure* means 'to convince someone, or to tell someone confidently that something can be relied on'.

envelop/envelope
Envelop is the verb, meaning 'to wrap up or surround', while *envelope* is one of those paper things you put letters in.

etc.
Etc. comes from the Latin 'et cetera', which means 'and the rest'. Because the *et* means 'and', you should never put the word *and* before it. And because the whole word has been shortened, it is best to put a point after it, to show it is an abbreviation. The word feels a bit lazy or dismissive, so it's best to avoid it if possible.

everyday/every day
The word *everyday* is an adjective, so use it when you're describing something – such as *an everyday occurrence*. Otherwise, separate the two words: 'I go for a walk every day.'

flare/flair
Flair means 'talent' – *she has a flair for marketing* – whereas an argument might *flare up*, like a fire.

flaunt/flout
Flaunt means 'to show off', and *flout* means 'to ignore conspicuously'. People tend to flaunt their wealth and flout the law, although it might be better if they did the opposite.

hoard/horde
A hoard is a very large collection of treasure, whereas a horde is a very large collection of unpleasant people, usually barbarians or savages.

imply/infer
When you imply something, you say it without spelling it out: *His answer implied that he was not enthusiastic about the job.* When you infer something, you work out what someone else is implying: *They inferred from his answer that he was not enthusiastic about the job.*

its/it's
It's is short for 'it is' or 'it has'. *Its* shows that something belongs to it. *It's a good dog that knows its master.*

licence/license
As with *advice* and *advise*, and *practice* and *practise*, *licence* is the noun and *license* is the verb. If you are licensed to drive a car, then you have a driving licence (not a driver's license, as in the US).

loathe/loath
If you are reluctant to do something, you are loath (or loth) to do it. If you really can't stand someone, you loathe them.

lose/loose
Lose (rhyming with shoes) means 'to misplace something'. *Loose* (rhyming with moose) is the opposite of tight.

metre/meter
When you meter something you measure it. A meter is something you use for measuring, such as a parking meter. A metre is a unit of length.

mis- words
Remember that the prefix added to words to show that they have been done wrongly or badly (misunderstand, miscount, misspell) has only a single *s*. New words beginning with *mis-* are quite often coined, and so they won't appear in your spellchecker for a while. A recent addition is *mis-sell*, as in *the recent scandals over mortgage and pensions mis-selling*.

mitigate/militate
Mitigate means 'soften or make less severe', as in *mitigating circumstances* – i.e. circumstances that make the crime less severe. *Militate* means the opposite – it comes from the same word as *military*, and literally means 'to serve as a soldier'. For example, *Its complexity militates against its success*. Never, ever use the phrase *mitigates against*.

pour/pore
When you study a book or report intently, you pore over it. Pouring over it would make the ink run.

practice/practise
The one with the *s* is the verb: you go to band practice in order to practise your instrument.

principle/principal

Principal means 'first or main', as in *the principal reason for our success*. Principle means 'something fundamental', as in a belief (*my principles won't allow me to steal*), a tenet (*the principle behind this is profit*) or an approach (*we agree with your idea in principle, but we'd like to make some changes*).

proscribe/prescribe

If you proscribe something, you forbid it. If you prescribe something, you authoritatively recommend it.

refute

Means 'disprove', rather than 'deny'.

reign/rein

Monarchs have reigns and horses have reins, but people often get them confused. There is no *g* in the kind of reins that gee-gees have, so you just have to work out which metaphor you are using. You might say *she took over the reins of the company* or *confusion reigned*.

respective

Respective and *respectively* mean 'in the order I mentioned them'. 'My mother and sister holidayed in France and Italy respectively' means that my mother went to France and my sister to Italy. Without the *respectively*, they would both have gone to both places. People often use the word just to mean 'their own', as in *they all returned to their respective houses*. Although this is correct, the sentence would mean exactly the same without *respective*. It is best to avoid these words altogether and change the sentence if necessary.

sat/sitting

Always say *he was sitting* rather than *he was sat*. No one would say *I was swam* rather than *I was swimming*, but lots of people make exactly this mistake with sitting – and with standing too.

sever/severe

Sever means 'to cut', *severe* means 'strict or serious'.

shear/sheer

You shear a sheep. All the other meanings are spelled *sheer*: 'sheer madness', 'a sheer drop', 'he sheered out of the way of the oncoming lorry'.

site/cite

Site means 'to put something (especially a building) in a particular place', while *cite* means 'to invoke an authority or other evidence to support a proposition'.

stationary/stationery

With an *a* it means 'not moving', with an *e* it means 'writing materials'. I remember it by the fact that the word *pen* has an *e* in it.

story/storey

If you mean the floor of a building, the spelling is *storey*. A *story* is a tale. American English spells both *story*.

their/there/they're
Their (possessive) coats are *there* (place), but *they're* (they are) all wet.

till/until
Till (with a double *l*) and *until* mean the same thing, but *until* tends to sound better at the beginning of a sentence. Because both these words exist, there is no need to use *'til*.

toe/tow
When you are forced to obey group discipline, you *toe the line* – like a soldier touching a line on the parade ground with his toes in order to keep the ranks straight. You don't *tow* it.

trust
As in *I trust this letter answers all your questions*. It is always presumptuous and often sounds sarcastic to use *I trust. I hope* is much better.

utilize/use
Utilize is one of those words people utilize when they want to sound important. I've never seen an example of it that couldn't be replaced by *use*, which is a much less pretentious word.

whose/who's
Who's means *who is*. *Whose* is the possessive. *Guess whose shoes these are, and guess who's coming to dinner.*

your/you're

You're is short for 'you are'; *your* shows something belongs to you: *You're trustworthy and your heart's in the right place.*

Confusing differences between British and US English

Because we in Britain are exposed to so much American media – books, films, TV programmes and computer programs – it is easy to forget that there are differences between American and British English. Using American English by mistake can easily alienate or confuse your readers – as can using British English if you are writing for American readers.

The intention of this section is to give you a list of things to check, to make sure that you don't use American English when British would be more appropriate – or vice versa.

Word endings
-eable/-able (sizeable/sizable)
British English: Keep the *e*.
American English tends to drop the *e* in words like *likeable*, whereas British English retains it. American English also drops the e from words like *judgement*.

-ae/-e (aesthetic/esthetic)
British English: Keep the *a*.
American English tends to drop the *a* from words like *aesthetic* and *paediatrician*, whereas British English keeps it.

-ce/-se (licence/license)
British English: Use -se for a verb, -ce for a noun.
American English ends some words with -se that we always end with -ce, such as *defence*. In British English, nouns that end -ce, like *the licence*, change their endings to -se when they become verbs, like *to license*. In American English, words never change in this way: verb and noun both end in -se.

-ise/-ize and -yse/-yze (baptise/baptize and analyse/ analyze)
British English: Always use an *s*.
In British English there are a large number of words (such as *baptize* and *realize*) that end either with -ize or with -ise. Some British publishers spell all of them with -ise, whereas others (including Penguin) spell some of them with -ize, to reflect the route by which they came into English. For most people, it is easiest to use the -ise spelling, since it is always allowable, and it gives you one less thing to remember. If you do choose to use -ize endings, make sure you are consistent throughout your document. In American English, the -ize endings are not optional – you have to get them right. However, a spellchecker set to use American English will pick them all up for you.

In American English, some words end in -yze (such as *analyze*) that are always spelled -yse in British English.

-our/-or (colour/color)
British English: Keep the *u*.
American English usually drops the *u* from words like *colour* and *favour*.

-re/-er (theatre/theater)
British English: Use *-re*.
American English often switches round the letters *re* so that words such as *theatre* and *centre* become *theater* and *center*. This makes the spelling closer to the pronunciation, but we've never cared much for that in Britain.

Spelling differences
There are plenty of words that have different spellings or meanings in British and American English, such as *suspenders*, which are for Americans what the British call *braces*, but which are for the British what Americans call *garters*. However, only a few of these are likely to cause trouble in the office:

cheque/check
In British English, you use a cheque to pay and a check to verify. American English uses *check* for both purposes.

got/gotten
British English: Don't use *gotten*.
Only American English uses *gotten* as the past participle of *get*. In British English, we say *got*: *I have got a cold* rather than *I have gotten a cold*. The only exception is in the phrase *ill-gotten gains*.

oblige/obligate
British English: Use *oblige*.
In American English, you would say *The Senate's rules obligate its members to convene a trial*. In British English, you would use the word *oblige*.

programme/program
British English: Use *programme* unless you're talking about a piece of software.
In British English you would have a *programme of events* or a *television programme* but a *word-processing program*. American English uses *program* in all senses.

sceptical/skeptical
British English: Use *sceptical*.
In American English this is spelt with a *k*, but in British English it has a *c*.

titbit/tidbit
British English: Use *titbit*.
   Although the word comes from an English dialect word *tid*, meaning 'tender or nice', the standard form in British English is now *titbit*, whereas American English uses *tidbit*. As with *gotten*, American English often retains older features that have since disappeared from British English.

transport/transportation
British English: Use *transport*.
When talking generally about moving things around, American English prefers *transportation*, but the shorter word *transport* means the same thing in British English, and is much more familiar.

The only sure way to guard against mistakes is to suspect all of your words. If you have the slightest doubt about a word, look it up in a dictionary – even if you've looked it up before. It won't take long for you to get a good sense of the meanings of the most often confused words. This will make you a more confident writer, and thus a better one.

Jargon and buzzwords

There are some words and phrases that people often use at work, but which risk alienating their readers. People outside your industry (and a surprising number inside it) may not understand the jargon you use, and buzzwords can make you sound unoriginal.

Here are some to look out for, with suggestions for alternatives:

pick the low-hanging fruit	*deal with the easiest targets first* Or make up your own metaphor.
let's take it offline	*let's discuss or deal with it privately or informally*
the helicopter view	*an overview*
establish a level playing field	*make things fair*
a win-win situation	Say how it benefits both parties. This term comes from game theory, which studies the different outcomes of games. The best outcome is victory for both players: win-win, rather than win-lose. If the best outcome really has been achieved, then say so.

a zero-sum game	This also comes from game theory. It means a game in which victory for one player automatically means defeat for the other.
our core competencies	*the things we're best at*
a steep learning curve	*learning a lot quickly*
key learnings	*important lessons*
a step change	*an enormous change* Or some other description of the change – ideally a specific one. A step change can either be one in small increments or one in which everything changes fundamentally. The latter comes from a marketing analysis of political, economic, social and technological factors – called a PEST or STEP analysis.
downsizing	*laying people off* Since everyone knows what this is a euphemism for, you may at least get credit for being honest. The same goes for many of the terms here.
paradigm shift	*a completely new way of looking at things* If you genuinely have a

completely new way of looking at things, then simply describing it will be enough. Anything less than that isn't a paradigm shift. Either way, there's no need for this phrase.

leveraging	*using* or *making better use of*
synergy	This is what happens when the combined effect of things is greater than the sum of their individual effects. It is better to spell out how this will happen than to sum it up with this word, which is often used incorrectly.
empowering	*giving more power to* It is better to identify the power and say how it will increase.
leading-edge	*leading* Leading-edge is quite dated now, and didn't mean much in the first place.
think outside the box	If you use a cliché to describe creative thinking you are probably not going to get very far.
blue-skies thinking	As above.

Index

abbreviations (including acronyms) 111–13, 182
use of apostrophes in 193
abstraction 121–4
Accenture 171
acronyms *see* abbreviations
actions 106, 132–42, 160
actualize 139
adverbs 217
adverse/averse 223
advice/advise 223
affect/effect 138, 223
agendas, catering for different 22
Aitchison, Jean 16
Algeria's oil production, example using 166–8
Allen, Robert 181
allude 223
alternate/alternative 223
ampersand (&) 209
and, beginning a sentence with 171
annual report example 33–5
apology, importance of 152
apostrophes 192–5
appendices 61, 70
appraise/apprise 137, 224
argument 39, 41, 64
Armchair Economist, The 18
article 70
Articulate Mammal, The 16

as such 122
assure/ensure/insure 226
attachments to emails 54
audience 1, 94
apparent 24
false 24
focusing on the most important part 23
individual 22
mass 22
multiple 29
segments 22
auditors 23
aural/oral 224
authority, air of 154
averse vs *adverse* 223

bartleby.com 187
bcc line, use of in emails 52
benefits of writing well 103
betwixt 186
biographies, use of in proposals 66
block *see* writer's block
blue-skies thinking 239
bought/brought 224
box, thinking outside the 239
brackets 194
square 81
British English/US English 233–7
brochures 72–3

brought/bought 224
Bryson, Bill 18
bullet-points 171–6
buzzwords 141, 237–9

*Cambridge Encyclopaedia of the
    English Language* 188
can 136
capital letters 183, 185, 209–12
    common mistakes with 212
cc line, use of in emails 52
cheque/check 235
Chomsky, Noam 17
chose/choose 224
Churchill, Winston S. 5, 221
cite/site 231
clauses 219–20
Cloze procedure 15
collaboration *see* team working
colons 196
commas 197–9
    use of with *that* and *which*
        214
company, terms specific to
    your 108
compare to/compare with 224
complaints, answering 148–53
complement 134
compliment/complement 225
comprise 225
conceptualize 139
conclusion, in article 70
confidence 153–7
    common strategies for
        dealing with lack of xii
contents, table of 57, 93
continual/continuous 225
contributors 91

control 163
conventions 209–21
Cooper, Alan 27
core competency 141, 238
could 136
councillor/counsellor 225
cover of report 56
covering letter 64
creative writing 101
credentialize 139
criticism, constructive *see*
        feedback
Crystal, David 187–8
cue, importance of taking
    from client 63
curricula vitae 75–6
customer base 121–2

dashes 199–201
dates, conventions in letters 48
decades, use of apostrophes in
    193
defuse/diffuse 225
deleting, importance of not 82
deliverable 141
departments 109
design of documents 94
dictionaries 88, 93, 137, 181–3
directness 136
discreet/discrete 226
discussion, in article 70
disinterested/uninterested 226
distractions 84
downsizing 238
drafts 82, 86, 94
    first 93
draw/drawer 226
drive 140

e.g./i.e. 226
Economist Style Guide, The 185
Economist, The 18
editing marks 181, 190–91
editing on screen 83
effect/affect 138, 223
elegance 101
Elements of Style, The 187
emails 51–4
  layout of 51
  coldness of 53
emphasis, use of quotation
  marks for 205
empowering 239
Enron, strength of brand 144
ensure/insure/assure 226
enthusiasm, excessive 148
envelop/envelope 227
ergo 186
ERTMS (European Rail Traffic
  Management System)
  112–16
etc. 227
everyday/every day 227
examples
  focusing on the most
    important part of your
    audience 23
  of annual report 33–5
  of unsolicited sales letter 27,
    145–6
  using Algeria's oil
    production 166–8
  using Guernsey 133
  using Shire Pharmaceuticals
    159–62
  using Strategic Rail
    Authority 112–16, 153

using VPN (Virtual Private
  Network) article 42–4
exclamation marks 148, 189, 201
executive summary 58, 66, 93
extravert personality type 6–7
eye fixations 13

FAQs (frequently asked
  questions) 75
feedback 88, 91, 92
feeling personality type 6, 8
fees, setting out in proposals
  69
Fergusson, Rosalind, Martin
  Manser and David
  Pickering 184
Financial Times 18
flare/flair 227
flaunt/flout 227
flow 116
  in short sentences 170
forewords 58
Fowler, Henry Watson 187
Fowler's Modern English Usage,
  The New 186
full stops 202–3
FYI (for your information),
  use of in emails 54

gesture 150
glossaries 61
goal dictates message 33
goals of writing 1, 31
  as a table 32
got/gotten 235
grammar
  guides 181, 187–8
  teaching of xi

Green, Dr Georgia 10
greetings
  in emails 53
  in letters 48
Guardian 185
Guernsey, example using 133

habits 3
Hayes, John R. 29
he/she and *they* 215–16
helicopter view 237
Heller, Richard 71
High Impact Speeches 71
hoard/horde 228
hook, use of in article 70
Horning, Alice 6
house style 185
How the Mind Works 18
human, importance of
  sounding 152
hyphens 186, 203

I/me 212–13
i.e./e.g. 226
IBM, poetic nature of 144
ice-breakers, use of in emails
  53
imagination, use of 29
impact, as a verb 138
imply/infer 228
incentivize 139
information, essential in any
  sentence 102
initialisms *see also*
  abbreviations 111
*Inmates Are Running the
  Asylum, The* 27
Innovator's Advantage, The 171

insincerity 148
insure/assure/ensure 226
Internet resources 181
introvert personality type
  6–7
intuitive personality type 6,
  7–8
it 129
its/it's 228
its/it's 193
ITT (invitation to tender) 63
-ize words 139

jargon 16, 108, 237–9
Jensen, George H. and
  DiTiberio, John K. 6
judging personality type 6,
  8–9
Jung, Carl G. 6

Kim, W. Chan and
  Mauborgne, Renee 105
King's English, The 187
KISS (keep it short and
  simple) principle 162

Landsburg, Stephen 18
Latin 217
layout
  of documents 94
  of emails 51
  of letters 47
leader, when writing in teams
  90
leading-edge 239
leaflets, demands and
  conventions of 74
learning curve 238

learnings 238
letters 46–51
  final paragraph of 50
  first paragraph of 49
  layout of 47
  tone of 50
leveraging 239
licence/license 228
linguistics 16
linking information, four ways
  of 39
lists 119
literacy demands on job-
  holders ix
loathe/loath 228
lose/loose 228
low-hanging fruit 237

Making Sense of Grammar 187
Matalene, Dr Carolyn ix
MBA (Masters of Business
  Administration) students,
  trying to teach xiii
me/I 212–13
measures 194
medium 46–76
memory, short-term 120
messages 1
  conveying 35
  definition of 33
  dictated by goal 33
  in article 70
  managing multiple 34
  most important in the
    whole book 20
method for planning and
  writing 1
metre/meter 229

Microsoft Word, 'Track
  changes' feature of 95
Microsoft's Grammar Check
  214
mis- words 229
mitigate/militate 229
Myers-Briggs Type Indicator 6

names 108
needs and responses,
  articulating in proposals
  66
newspaper, being a one-man 78
non-fiction, accessible 18
noun 136
numbering pages of a report 57
numbers 214

objects 213, 220
oblige/obligate 235
Office Angels, survey
  conducted by 141
offices 109
offline, taking it 237
operationalize 139
optimize 139, 140
oral/aural 224
order, chronological and
  narrative 39, 40
overcomplicate, the urge to xiv
overused words 4

pact between readers and
  writers 15
padding 133
paradigm shift 238
paragraphs, standard 151
passive sentences 124–8

acceptable reasons for using
127
pen and paper 83
Penguin Dictionary, The 181
Penguin Thesaurus, The 184
people 108
  importance of in writing
  106
perceiving personality type 6,
  8–9
personality types 6–9
personality, relation to writing
  of 6
personas, use of by software
  developers 26
phrases, stock 151
Pinker, Steven 18
planning 1
playing field, level 237
points of view, catering for
  different 22
politics, office 90
pour/pore 229
pp (per procurationem), use of
  in letters 49
practice/practise 229
prepositions 213, 219, 220
press releases 70
'prewrite, write, rewrite',
  approach to writing 7
principle/principal 230
profiling of readers 21
programme/program 236
project manager 90
projects
  how to run 96
  major 88
  minor 86

proofreaders' marks 190–91
proposals, demands and
  conventions of *see also*
  reports 62–70
proscribe/prescribe 230
*Psycholinguistics of Readable
  Writing, The* 6
punctuation 176, 192–208
  in quotations 206

qualifiers, overuse of 154
question marks 204
quotation marks 185, 205
quotations, use of 71

railways, example using 112–16
reader profile 21–7
  how to fill in 25
  how to use 28
readers *see also* audience 1,
  20–30
  actions required of 1, 31, 36
  fast 11
  slow 11
reading 9–18
  aloud 12
  speed and writing style 9
  style 9
reasonable, importance of
  sounding 152
recommendations 153–7
references 194, 196
refute 230
reign/rein 230
reports, demands and
  conventions of 55–61
respective 230
respectively 186

reviewers 91
RFP (request for proposals) 63
roles
    importance of clear 88
    making writing easier 78
rules 209–21
    unwritten, of writing 15, 18

sales letters, unsolicited 27
sales pitches 145–7
sat/sitting 231
sceptical/skeptical 236
scrapbook 82
semicolons 207
sensing personality type 6,
    7–8
sentences
    active 125
    beginning 221
    beginning with *and* 171
    complex 164–6
    ending 221
    ensuring each has a verb 169
    essential information in 102
    full 169
    guidelines for clear 128
    ideal length 169
    length of 106, 159–78
    not focusing on one thing
        129
    overgrown 166–8
    passive 124–8
    reducing length of 167
    short 163
    structure of 166
    stunted 169–171
    what they must do 102
    within sentences 164–6

sever/severe 231
sexist language 215
shear/sheer 231
*Short History of Nearly
    Everything, A* 18
Shire Pharmaceuticals,
    example using 159–62
signatures
    in emails 54
    in letters 49
sign-offs
    in emails 53
    in letters 48
simplicity 162
site/cite 231
situation in which your writing
    will be read 27
skimming, style of reading 11
Skinner, B. F. 17
spaces 208
speech, use of quotation marks
    in 205–7
speed reading 12–15
    exercise 14
spellchecking software 222
spelling 222–32
split infinitives 217–18
splurging 80
sports reports, effect on
    reading styles 10–11
sprints, reading 14
square brackets 81
standfirst 70
stationary/stationery 231
statistics, use of 71
step change 238
story 39, 40
story/storey 231

story, turning writing into a 17
strapline 35
Strategic Rail Authority (SRA),
    examples using 112–16,
    153
strategize 139
strengths
    identifying 4
    using in proposals 63
structure 1, 38–45
    importance of explaining 41
    of sports reports 10–11
    purpose of 38
    summarizing and reordering
    42–4
Strunk, William 187
style guides 88, 93, 181, 185–6
subject line, use of in emails 52
subjects 105–31, 134, 212, 220
    confusing 119
    introducing 107
subvocalizing 9, 13
summarizing 42–4
summary *see also* executive
    summary 36
synergy 139, 141, 239
synonyms 184

tasks, breaking writing down
    into 1
tautology 155
team working 86–99
team, describing in proposals
    66
terms, unexplained 108
that/which 214
their/there/they're 231
theme 39, 40

thesauruses 181, 184
they 129
they and *he/she* 215–16
thinking personality type 6, 8
till/until 232
Times, The 185
titbit/tidbit 236
titles
    of documents 35
    royal, aristocratic and
    military 185
    use of capitals in 211
    use of quotation marks for
    205
to line, use of in emails 52
toe/tow 232
tone 143–58
    of letters 50
    of proposals 62
touch-typing 83
'Track changes' *see* Microsoft
    Word, 'Track changes'
    feature of
transport/transportation 236
trust 151, 232
typing 83

uninterested/disinterested 226
until/till 232
US English/British English
    233–7
usage 182
usage guides 181, 186–7
utilize/use 139, 232

verbs *see also* actions 134
    ensuring every sentence has
    one 169

version control 94
versions 86
Visigoth 183
voice, using as an aid to
    editing 181, 188–90
VPN (Virtual Private
    Network) article, example
    using 42–4

weaknesses, identifying your 4
webpages, demands and
    conventions of 74–5
what, action of sentence *see
    also* actions; verbs 102
which/that 214
who/whom 218–20
who, subject of sentence *see
    also* subjects 102
whose/who's 193, 232

win-win 141, 237
words
frequently confused 138,
    223–32
  unnecessary, new or made-
    up 138–41
  wasted 167
  wrong 137–8
workplan 108
would 136
would potentially 155
writer, when writing in teams
    89
writer's block 79
writing for yourself 29

your/you're 232

zero-sum game 238